THE LAST CIVIL RIGHTS MOVEMENT

DIANE DRIEDGER

The Last
Civil Rights
Movement

Disabled Peoples' International

HURST & COMPANY, LONDON

ST. MARTIN'S PRESS, NEW YORK

Printed in the United Kingdom by
C. Hurst & Co. (Publishers) Ltd.,
38 King Street, London WC2E 8JT,
and in the United States of America by
St. Martin's Press, Inc.,
175 Fifth Avenue, New York, NY 10010.
All rights reserved.
© Diane Driedger, 1989
Printed in England on long-life paper

ISBNs

Hurst cased: 1–85065–044–6
Hurst paper: 1–85065–059–4

St. Martin's cased: 0–312–02834–2
St. Martin's paper: 0–312–02836–9

Library of Congress Cataloging-in-Publication Data

Driedger, Diane.
    The last civil rights movement / Diane Driedger.
        p.   cm.
    Bibliography: p.
    Includes index.
    ISBN 0-312-02834-2 : $39.00 (est.). -- ISBN 0-312-02836-9 (pbk.) :
    $19.95 (est.)
    1. Disabled Peoples' International. 2. Handicapped--Government
    policy. 3. Handicapped--Civil rights.   I. Title.
    HV1551.D74 1989
    362.4'048--dc19   89-4194
                                                              CIP

To disabled people and their allies in the self-help movement everywhere

PREFACE AND ACKNOWLEDGEMENTS

On a July night in 1980, in a room full of people with all kinds of disabilities, I had little awareness of the importance of the decision to forge an international organization of disabled people. Attending as a nondisabled worker, handing out papers, pouring water for speakers, I was caught up in wondering whether to give printed material to blind people, and hoped I would say the right thing. People were ecstatic at the decision to set up this new world body, Disabled Peoples' International (DPI). But having just worked for two months on a government summer student grant with the Manitoba League of the Physically Handicapped, I did not think of future ramifications. A year later Henry Enns, the chairperson of the Steering Committee to establish DPI, greeted me in a telephone conversation with, "How would you like to go to Singapore?" Thus I became a volunteer with the Mennonite Central Committee to help DPI organize its founding world congress in Singapore in 1981.

This book tells the story of how disabled people have organized themselves to speak out for their own rights in over seventy countries. It was not completed without struggle, because I discovered in the process of preparing it that many people do not consider the history of disabled people to be very important. I was told that I should have been studying in the Social Work, Sociology or Medical faculties where "the problems of disabled people belong." But I argue that disabled people have a distinctive history, and that this should be written and reflected upon. People with disabilities are not merely clients, patients or deviants to be dealt with by professional practitioners in the fields of social work, medicine and sociology. Disabled people's history and their struggle for participation are beginning to be recognized by society at large.

This book, I hope, will serve to promote awareness of the goals and abilities of disabled people. Furthermore, it is important for disabled people to know their own history, just as it has been so crucial for all oppressed groups – black people, colonized peoples, women and others – to learn about themselves. This is an account of how disabled people built an international organization to represent themselves and to demand their rights as citizens of the world. I hope it will be a useful tool for disabled persons to reflect on their past struggle and to formulate strategies for the future.

Acknowledgements

This book, which began as a Master's thesis, could not have been completed without the openness and cooperation of many people. My thanks are due to those who consented to be interviewed, and those who responded to my letters of inquiry. I also acknowledge the cooperation of the Disabled Peoples' International (DPI) Development Program Office in Winnipeg, which provided access to DPI documents and assisted financially with mailing and photocopying costs. The help of translators was particularly important, and in this connection I thank Francisco Valenzuela (Spanish), Richard Bueddefeld-Noël (French), Victor Moreira (Portuguese), and Heidi Harms and Ernest Ens (German). Thanks are due to April D'Aubin, Agnes Hubert, Doreen Martens, Leona Penner and Jim Derksen for their suggestions; the input and encouragement of Henry Enns, DPI chairperson, proved invaluable. I appreciated working with Professor T.E. Vadney of the History Department, University of Manitoba, who was my Master's thesis advisor; he was willing to direct a topic which was little known. Finally, my thanks to my husband Ted Ens, whose encouragement spurred me on.

Kingston, Jamaica   D.D.
Fall 1988

CONTENTS

ABBREVIATIONS

ACCD	American Coalition of Citizens with Disabilities
BCODP	British Council of Organizations of Disabled People
CADIS	Corporación Argentina de Discapacidados
CBR	Community-Based Rehabilitation
CDA	Combined Disabilities Association
CIDA	Canadian International Development Agency
CIL	Centre for Independent Living
COPOH	Coalition of Provincial Organizations of the Handicapped (Canada)
CRCD	Canadian Rehabilitation Council for the Disabled
DPI	Disabled Peoples' International
DPSA	Disabled People South Africa
ECOSOC	(UN) Economic and Social Council
FIMITIC	Fédération Internationale des Mutilés, des Invalides du Travail et des Invalides Civils
HCK	Handicappförbundens Centralkommitté (Sweden)
ICOD	International Council on Disability
IFB	International Federation of the Blind
ILO	International Labor Organization
ILSMH	International League of Societies for Persons with Mental Handicap
IMPACT	International Initiative Against Avoidable Disablement
IYDP	International Year of Disabled Persons
MCC	Mennonite Central Committee (Canada)
MI	Mobility International
NCDPZ	National Council of Disabled Persons of Zimbabwe
NFB	National Federation of the Blind (USA)
ORD	Organization of Disabled Revolutionaries (Nicaragua)
RI	Rehabilitation International
UN	United Nations
UNESCO	UN Educational, Scientific and Cultural Organization
UNHPM	Union Nationale des Handicapés Physiques et Mentaux de Mauritanie
WCPD	World Coalition of People with Disabilities
WCWB	World Council for Welfare of the Blind
WAFAH	West African Federation for the Advancement of Handicapped Persons
WFD	World Federation of the Deaf
WHO	World Health Organization
WPA	World Program of Action Concerning Disabled Persons

1

INTRODUCTION

"We are mobilizing for what, hopefully, will be the last great civil rights struggle, and those who oppose us will be swept from the stage of history and become mere shadows of the past."[1]

— Liam Maguire (Ireland), 1981

Many disabled people view their rights movement as the last in a long series of movements for rights – labor, blacks, colonized peoples, poor people, women – and now people with disabilities. Indeed, it appears that disabled people are some of the last people to be engaged in this historical sweep of the struggle for human rights. Even in places where some groups of disabled people organized relatively early, such as in Sweden in the late nineteenth century, other oppressed groups have organized before them. As of the 1980s, disabled people all over the world have taken up the struggle for equality and participation on an equal footing with other citizens.

Organizations composed entirely of persons with various disabilities – physical, mental and sensory – have sprung up in 100 countries since the mid-1970s. Disabled people have come to a realization that their societies were built without their input and participation. One of the results of this recognition was a gathering of disabled people in Singapore in 1981 to form Disabled Peoples' International (DPI). DPI's mandate is to be the voice of disabled people and it believes that disabled people should be integrated into society and participate with the same rights as everyone else. With membership in sixty-nine countries, it is activist-oriented, it looks to lobby governments and the UN, and it educates the public about the aspirations and abilities of disabled people. Its members hold that by speaking unitedly they are stronger than when each disability group speaks out on its own concerns. It has been granted consultative status with the United Nations, the United Nations Educational, Scientific and Cultural Organization (UNESCO), and the International Labour Organization. While local, national and regional organizations have existed since 1945, DPI is the first successful effort of people of various disabilities to create a united voice at the international level.

1

DPI was formed to express the views of the 10 per cent of the world's population who are disabled in one way or another. There were over 500 million disabled people worldwide in 1985.[2] Disabled people have a physical, mental, or sensory impairment, and their "handicap is the loss or limitation of opportunities to take part in the normal life of the community on an equal level with others due to physical or social barriers."[3]

In the 1980s, the majority of disabled persons, 80 per cent, resided in the developing world – Africa, Asia, the Middle East, Latin America and the Caribbean. In some countries the incidence of disability due to malnutrition and communicable diseases was estimated at 20 per cent of the population.[4] Disabled people, whether in developed or developing countries, are usually poor. This poverty stems from a lack of opportunities to work and participate in the mainstream of society. DPI affirms that disabled people want to work and live in the community as do nondisabled people. This view has arisen out of disabled people's experiences since 1945.

By the 1960s and 1970s, people with disabilities began to question society's definition of them as odd and abnormal or as so-called cripples. They rejected the tendency of sociologists, social workers and doctors to label them as deviants, clients and patients. They became aware that society's attitude towards them, the idea that disabled people should be shut away from nondisabled society, was a handicap. Disabled people reminded everyone that all people were mortal and vulnerable to physical and mental disabilities. Furthermore, because disabled people had been warehoused in institutions and shut away in parental homes, they had no input into the design of society's streets, buildings, sidewalks and work places. Many disabled people could not participate fully in society because they could not even enter most buildings. There were stairs or narrow doorways where wheelchair-users could not enter. If mobility-impaired people could not enter buildings, they could not attend university, hold down a job, or find a place to live outside an institution. Without education and income, disabled people could not become independent and enter the mainstream of society.

Disabled people, realizing these things, ceased blaming themselves for their limitations. They had internalized the attitudes of nondisabled society towards them.[5] They began to see themselves as powerful and beautiful people who had something to contribute to society.

Literature about disabled people abounds and its many genres reflect attitudes towards disabled persons. Professionals in the areas of psychology, sociology, medicine and social work write about disabled persons as patients and subjects of study. Popular authors tell personal stories about disabled people who overcame their misfortunes and triumphed in life. Other literature focusses on the social situation of disabled people and proposes solutions. Most of these accounts have been written by nondisabled people.

While a few disabled people have written about themselves, they are often only writing their own personal stories. They do not recount the story of all of their sisters and brothers. But a new area of literature has opened up in the last ten years. Disabled people are starting to write about themselves as a collective body of people and to propose solutions for the barriers to equality in their lives. Moreover, this literature does not only reflect the opinions and observations of a single author. It is representative of the philosophies and views of a mass of disabled persons, who have united into self-help organizations. It reflects disabled people's push for their full participation and equality in society.

Finkelstein and Enns, both disabled, write about society's attitudes towards disabled people and how these attitudes have interacted with the growing demand for change expressed by disabled persons.[6] They view environmental and attitudinal barriers as the reason why disabled individuals are unable to participate, rather than their disabilities. Society, however, still views people with disabilities as sick, helpless patients who need to be cared for. Enns and Finkelstein assert that disabled people's organizations are working to inform society about its attitudes and to help integrate disabled persons into the mainstream of life.

Much of the writing by disabled people is in reaction to professionals, who after the Second World War began to study and postulate about disabled persons. Returning war veterans who became disabled in the war and survivors of the polio epidemics of the 1940s and 1950s were rehabilitated with new medical techniques and began to live longer. Everything about their lives became the subject of professional investigation. Professionals, as a result, began to view disabled people as individuals with "problems", and accordingly disabled people's lack of participation in society is their personal problem. For example, medical professionals write about the physical rehabilitation techniques needed for different disabling conditions and they discuss how disabling conditions affect everyday physical functioning in society. How disabled people eat, sleep, talk, move around and cope emotionally with their physical "problem" is discussed.[7]

Three branches of the disabled people's movement have emerged since

1970: the independent living movement, consumer organizations, and self-help groups. Independent living involves disabled people living and participating in the community like everyone else. Disabled people themselves control the boards of Independent Living Centers, formed mainly in Canada, Britain and the United States to help disabled individuals set up the services they need to live in the community. This is of particular use to disabled persons with more severe disabilities who may require services such as an attendant, a helper to assist in personal care.[8]

Unlike Independent Living Centers, consumer organizations of disabled people generally do not provide services. They monitor existing services provided by governments and non-profit rehabilitation organizations. And they believe that such organizations should be multidisability. Consumer organizations are a Western world phenomenon and a reaction to the fact that rehabilitation professionals have made decisions for disabled people in the past. Disabled people, through their organizations, now monitor the quality of their own services, such as rehabilitation, transportation and housing. These organizations assert that disabled persons have rights as citizens to services that enhance an independent living lifestyle.[9]

Independent Living Centers sometimes influence governmental policies for all disabled people in their area (depending on the center), while consumer organizations do not provide services. But a third type of organization both influences governments and agencies and provides services where they are needed. Self-help organizations of disabled people have emerged all over the world since the mid-1970s. Particularly in the developing world, where there were no Independent Living Centers, disabled people formed self-help organizations to lobby governments and to provide services such as rehabilitation, technical aids (wheelchairs, braces, crutches and white canes), housing and employment. Disabled Peoples' International is an international organization which includes mostly consumer and self-help groups.

While some research has been done on DPI and its national affiliates, there are few published works and there is little writing that provides an extensive history of the movement. This book is an attempt to do so. And it is different from most other writing that exists about disabled people. Most who have written about disabled people present them as clients, patients and objects of study and marvel. Relatively few of the authors have been disabled people themselves or allies of the disabled people's movement. In contrast, this book is written by an ally, and based mainly on letters and written reports by disabled people, and interviews with disabled people themselves about their movement. Indeed, this is the story of a movement for change where disabled people themselves prove that they are not helpless patients and cripples who have no control over their own destiny; they are actors with dignity, not passive recipients of charity.

NOTES

1 Liam Maguire, "Development and Strengthening of Disabled Self-Help Organizations", address to Mobility International/Canadian Bureau for International Education Conference, "Living Together", at York University, Toronto, Canada, August 7, 1981, 1.

2 World Health Organization, "World-wide Estimates of the Magnitude of the Disability Problem, Its Causes and Future Trends", quoted in E. Helander, P. Mendis and G. Nelson, *Training the Disabled in the Community: An Experimental Manual on Rehabilitation and Disability Prevention for Developing Countries* (Geneva: WHO, 1980), P–7.

3 Disabled Peoples' International, "DPI Constitution", 1983, 1, DPI Development Office files, Winnipeg.

4 United Nations, *World Program of Action Concerning Disabled Persons* (New York: United Nations, 1983), 13.

5 Paulo Freire, *Pedagogy of the Oppressed* (New York: Seabury Press, 1970), 50 and 60. Through Freire's theory of "conscientization" a person realizes that he/she can transform the world and is not merely a passive, mute being as society sees the oppressed person. Once oppressed people can name their oppression and where it originates, they can move on to change their life situation.

6 Victor Finkelstein, *Attitudes and Disabled People: Issues for Discussion*, no. 5 (New York: World Rehabilitation Fund, 1980); Henry Enns, "Canadian Society and Disabled People: Issues for Discussion", *Canada's Mental Health* 40 (Dec. 1981), 14–17; Henry Enns, "The Historical Development of Attitudes Toward the Handicapped: A Framework for Change" in David S. Freeman and Barry Trute (*eds*), *Treating Families With Special Needs* (Ottawa: Canadian Association of Social Workers, 1981).

7 The following are some examples of this literature: Norman R. Bernstein, "Chronic Illness and Impairment", *Psychiatric Clinics of North America* (Aug. 1971), 331–46; Barney M. Dlin, Abraham Perlman and Evelyn Ringold, "Psychosexual Response to Ileostomy and Colostomy", *American Journal of Psychiatry* 126 (Sept. 1969), 374–81; and C. Murray Parkes and M.N. Napier, "Psychiatric sequelae of amputation", *British Journal of Hospital Medicine* (Nov. 1970), 610–14.

8 Gerben DeJong, "Independent Living: From Social Movement to Analytic Paradigm", *Archives of Physical Medicine and Rehabilitation* 60 (Oct. 1979), 435–46; Nancy M. Crewe and Irving Kenneth Zola, *Independent Living for Physically Disabled People* (San Fransisco: Jossey-Bass, 1983); Diane Driedger and April D'Aubin, "So You Want to Start an Independent Living Centre? A Winnipeg Case Study", *Caliper* XL (Dec. 1985), 14–16; Independent Living Resource Centre, *Independent*

Living for Persons with Disabilities in Canada, A Study Commissioned by the Secretariat on the Status of Disabled Persons, Dept. of the Secretary of State, Minister Responsible for the Status of Disabled Persons (Winnipeg: Independent Living Resource Centre, 1985); Val Regehr Richert, *Moving In . . . A Housing Manual* (Winnipeg: Independent Living Resource Centre, 1985); Barbara Hummel and Athonette Gilpatrick, *Peer Support Training Manual* (Wisconsin: Access to Independence, 1984).

9   Jim Derksen, *The Disabled Consumer Movement: Policy Implications for Rehabilitation Service Provision* (Winnipeg: Coalition of Provincial Organizations of the Handicapped [COPOH], 1980); Allan J. Simpson, *Consumer Groups: Their Organization and Function* (Winnipeg: COPOH, 1980); F.G. Bowe, J.E. Jacoby, L.D. Wisemen, *Coalition Building* (Washington, DC: American Coalition of Citizens with Disabilities [ACCD], 1978); Henry Enns, "Canadian Society and Disabled People"; Diane Driedger, "Speaking for Ourselves: A History of COPOH on its 10th Anniversary" in *Coalition of Provincial Organizations of the Handicapped 1985-86 Annual Report* (Winnipeg: COPOH, 1986); Jim Derksen, (ed.), *Report on a Open National Employment Conference* (Winnipeg: COPOH, 1978); COPOH, *Getting to Know COPOH* (Winnipeg: COPOH, 1985); Derek Fudge and Patty Holmes, *Together for Social Change: Employing Disabled Canadians* (Ottawa: National Union of Provincial Government Employees and COPOH, 1983).

2

IN THE WAKE OF CHANGE: POST-SECOND WORLD WAR DEVELOPMENTS, 1945–1980

"When I was fourteen, I got polio. When the doctor took my parents aside, my mother asked, 'Will he live?' The doctor looked at her and said, 'You should probably hope he dies, because if he lives he will be nothing more than a vegetable for the rest of his life.' Well, I'm here today as an artichoke. You know they're a little prickly on the outside with a big heart and I'd like to call on all the vegetables of the world to unite."[1]

— Ed Roberts (former director, California Dept. of Rehabilitation), 1983

The Second World War came and went and technological change accelerated in its wake. As a result, young people disabled by war, polio epidemics and accidents began to live longer. They were often segregated from the rest of society because disability professionals, such as doctors and social workers, labelled them as sick and different. Disabled young people soon realized that they wanted to participate in the world like everyone else. And while disabled persons in some parts of Europe had organized for their rights before 1939, most disabled people in the rest of the world began to organize in the 1960s and 1970s. Their desire for participation and equality with other citizens set the stage for DPI's entrance in 1980.

Technological changes and the growth of the rehabilitation professions

At the turn of the twentieth century, most disabled people were hidden from public view. In Western countries (Europe and North America), they were hidden away by their families, but they were also often housed in institutions for the so-called crippled, and asylums for the so-called mentally incompetent and deranged. In Africa, Asia, the Middle East, Latin America and the Caribbean, families hid their disabled members in their homes because funds were not available to build large institutions. Generally, the world viewed disabled people as unproductive burdens,

7

and persons with mental illness in particular were often viewed as possessed by demons.

The two World Wars began to change the lives of disabled people. After the First World War many young men wounded in the conflict, especially those with spinal cord injuries, did not survive because the technology to rehabilitate them was not yet available. It was only in the wake of the Second World War that industrialized countries began to improve medical rehabilitation techniques, which soon became available to the whole population. Young people with spinal cord injuries were living longer.[2] Many disabled people became more mobile as better wheelchairs and prosthetics (artificial limbs) were developed.

In addition to a increasingly large population of young people with spinal cord injuries, many young people and children became disabled due to the polio epidemics of the early 1950s in the Western world.[3] With improved rehabilitation techniques and machines such as the iron lung, many people survived the epidemics. Some people were quite severely disabled and relied on respirators and electric wheelchairs. Furthermore, children were born disabled due to thalidomide, the anti-morning sickness drug used by pregnant women in the late 1950s and early 1960s.[4] Finally, the disabled war veterans of the Vietnam War joined the ranks of young disabled persons.

Thus, in the post-1945 Western world, many disabled young people were living longer. And they had more mobility through improved technical aids. These young persons, greater in numbers than ever before, were generally not content to be locked away in institutions and nursing homes for the so-called crippled. After all, they had their whole lives in front of them. The post-1945 era, however, marked the rapid expansion of the rehabilitation professions, and institutions arose linked to the medical procedures needed to rehabilitate people physically. Medical professionals defined disabled people as sick people who spent their lives trying to get well. This view has served to influence society's attitude toward disabled people. It provided a rationale for excluding them from participation in society.[5] Since they were sick, they did not have to accept responsibility in everyday life; disabled people were already too busy getting well. Disabled people were seen to have suffered tragedies and as unable to care for themselves. They needed care, and institutions were places for this. Disabled people were seen as passive, needing others to make decisions for them because sick people did not need to take responsibility for themselves. Jim Derksen, a Canadian disabled activist, describes the effects of this stereotype as follows:

The disabled person is allowed less self-determination than what would normally be available to adults in his society, the disabled person is usually segregated from the participating majority in a treatment or recovery setting, he is made to feel lacking or defeated as he is most often unable to meet the chief responsibility given him of becoming well or able-bodied since most disabilities are permanent in nature.[6]

Because separate schools, housing and special services were established to care for disabled persons, nondisabled people had few opportunities to interact with disabled people as human beings with aspirations and emotions like themselves. The public saw disabled persons as those who needed a helping hand, and who needed money for medical research to be cured. People watched telethons for these medical causes and were often spurred to give money out of pity and often out of the fear that they too could become disabled. The public generally believed that normal life ended when one became disabled.

Early international organizations

In the 1950s, many parents, friends and other interested people realized that disabled young people needed services, such as specialized education (often separate schools were set up because disabled children could not climb the stairs of the public school) and activities to occupy themselves. These services would enable disabled people to live productive lives. Organizations of parents, friends and in some cases rehabilitation professionals sprang up in most Western countries. Ultimately international organizations were formed composed of national non-profit organizations interested in the prevention of disability and the integration into society of people with one disability or another.

All of these international organizations were 'uni-disability', i.e. focussed on a single disability. Few of them made concerted efforts to incorporate disabled people themselves in the membership, let alone the decision-making functions of the organizations.[7] In 1953, the Council of World Organizations Interested in the Handicapped (CWOIH, later the International Council on Disability), an umbrella organization of many of these international uni-disability concerned groups, was established. It was founded as a mechanism that member organizations could work through in cooperation to make presentations to the United Nations concerning rehabilitation.[8]

Around this time, however, disabled people themselves began to form national and international uni-disability organizations. They were determined to speak for themselves and to further the aims of disability prevention. Disabled people formed four international organizations: the World Federation of the Deaf (WFD), the International Federation of the Blind (later the World Blind Union), People First International, and the Fédération Internationale des Mutilés, des Invalides du Travail et des Invalides Civils (FIMITIC).

The World Federation of the Deaf was founded in 1951. Its aims were to prevent and treat deafness, to promote the growth of national organizations of deaf persons around the world, and to raise awareness about deafness.[9] It also had consultative status with the UN and other related agencies, the World Health Organization, the International Labor Organization and UNESCO. FIMITIC was founded in 1953. Its purpose was to bring together disabled people on common issues. Its membership was drawn mainly from Europe.[10]

The International Federation of the Blind (IFB) was important to the development of DPI because it provided some future leaders. The IFB had consultative status with the UN, and was composed of persons with visual impairments. It was born out of the World Council for the Welfare of the Blind (WCWB), founded in 1954. The WCWB, composed of both organizations of and for blind people, was dominated by organizations and institutions for visually handicapped people. One presenter jokingly remarked at a conference: "The organizations *for* the blind possess the resources and the emerging organizations *of* the blind the ideals."[11]

Differences over ideals, however, were no joke, as blind persons decided to separate from the WCWB and form their own federation consisting only of organizations made up of blind persons themselves. This split took place in New York in July 1964, at the World Assembly of the WCWB. Blind people had been organizing into their own self-help groups between 1960 and 1964, mostly in Asia and the United States. In fact, the National Federation of the Blind (NFB), formed in 1960 in the United States, was interested in enabling blind people in other countries to organize their own groups. Dr Isabella Grant of the NFB travelled to Asia and Africa to interest blind people in forming their own organizations.[12] Representatives of seven of these groups (from Pakistan, India, Malaysia, Hong Kong, Sri Lanka, Guatemala and the United States) attended the WCWB World Congress.[13] There they presented a resolution asking for at least half of WCWB national delegations to be composed of people who were themselves blind.[14] The majority of WCWB delegates voted against this resolution. Indeed, the delegates from organizations for blind persons did not understand the need for blind people to be equally represented in an organization that dealt with their concerns.

This defeat served as a catalyst for the organizations of blind people to form their own coalition. They met outside the regular WCWB Congress sessions in New York and formed the International Federation of the Blind, drafting a constitution stating that only organizations of blind persons could have voting power. It was to be an organization controlled by blind people. By 1974, the organization had members in forty-five countries in Europe, Asia, Africa and a few in Latin America.[15]

The WCWB and the IFB grew alongside each other for twenty years. The IFB had financial difficulties in holding World Congresses and in funding its operations. Both of the organizations received international recognition such as consultative status with the UN. In August 1984, the two organizations decided to unite into one "World Blind Union", a unified voice of and for blind people. An agreement was worked out, whereby the representation of blind people would be more than half in the decision-making bodies and national assemblies of the Union.[16]

In a parallel development, mentally handicapped people began organizing internationally in 1973. In that year in British Columbia, Canada, mentally handicapped people and some social workers met at a convention sponsored by the British Columbia Association for Retarded Citizens. As a result, a group called "People First" was organized in Portland, Oregon, in 1974.[17] The organization gained members in forty-one states of the USA, and it became a national organization. Mentally handicapped people formed the organization to speak out for their rights, asking to live in the community rather than in institutions. They had "helpers", often staff persons in institutions, who aided in the organizing of the groups. Throughout the late 1970s People First organizations were started in Canada and Sweden, thus ultimately forming People First International.

National and regional organizations of disabled people: Pre-1980

Organizations of disabled people started all over the world, in local and national chapters, throughout the late 1960s and 1970s. In some European countries disabled people had been organized since the late 1800s. But in North America the 1960s and its political climate of social change spurred disabled people to organize in the same way as blacks, poor people and women were doing. Disabled persons in nations emerging from colonialism, with poor economies, were not exempt from organizing. In fact, decolonization in Africa, in particular, spurred the development of disabled persons' organizations.

The developing world

AFRICA

By the 1980s there were more than 50 million disabled people in Africa.[18] Sixty per cent of African citizens were considered undernourished, which was a major cause of disability. Deficiencies in Vitamin A, in particular, led to blindness. Diseases such as polio and river blindness were common, and even though polio had been virtually wiped out in the industrialized countries through the Salk vaccine, most people in Africa did not have access to immunization. This was partly due to lack of government health resources to make vaccines available. In addition, many women were disabled as a result of the practise of female circumcision in many countries in Africa. The practise of removing the clitoris and/or the labia was frequently performed for cultural and religious reasons by village women in unsanitary conditions. Resulting disabilities included chronic pelvic pain and urinary tract infections, mental illness due to the trauma of undergoing the procedure and even mobility impairments.[19]

Generally, disabled people have been the most destitute of Africans. The main targets of disabling conditions were the poorest of Africans who lived in rural areas and the shantytowns of the big cities. Government planners have tended to emphasize the needs of the majority, and thus they have ignored the needs of disabled people and their families. Disabled people generally did not work in a mainstream job because there was high unemployment among nondisabled people in Africa already. Most disabled people supported themselves by begging in the big cities, or charitable institutions supported them.[20]

There were few services or structures to prevent disability or to rehabilitate disabled people and these few were centered in big cities. Thus they benefited a very small percentage of the disabled population because the majority of African people lived in rural areas.

African society's attitudes toward disabled people tended to be contradictory. Society attempted to integrate everyone into its workings and assigned each person a role, even a disabled person. But society also held some beliefs and myths that linked disability to sins committed either by disabled persons themselves or by their parents. Families saw disability as something to be ashamed of and this shame could bring about the killing of disabled children or the exile of their parents. In addition, disabled women were in a situation of double jeopardy. African society already accorded women a lower status than men. Thus, disabled women faced discrimination because they were women, and because they were disabled.[21]

With the dawn of the 1980s, disabled people started to form self-help groups to work for changes in society. Wars of liberation from oppressive governments and colonialism from the 1940s through the 1970s set the stage for disabled people's struggle for freedom and independence. After all, the rhetoric of freedom was already in everyone's vocabulary as nations freed themselves from British, French, Portuguese and Italian rule. In addition, many people became disabled as a result of liberation wars.

Disabled people's self-help organizations slowly became involved in solving the barriers to their participation in society. Organizations of disabled people arose in almost all African countries. These were both uni-disability, most often blind people's groups, and also national multi-disability groups. In most African countries organizations were founded in the cities, and there were difficulties in forming branches in the rural areas where the majority of disabled people lived.[22] Organizations of disabled people received little or no funding from their governments, and thus they relied on non-governmental development aid agencies from the West.[23]

Countries such as Mauritania and Zimbabwe had organizations that benefited from development agency funding. Ultimately, a West African regional coalition was forged with the help of Goodwill Industries of America, an organization concerned with employment options for disabled people. Disabled leaders from these organizations were to help in the formation of DPI.

Organizations of people of all disability groups sprang up in several West African countries in the middle and late 1970s. The National Union of Physically and Mentally Handicapped persons of Mauritania (Union Nationale des Handicapés Physiques et Mentaux de Mauritanie [UNHPM]) was founded in 1976. It was organized on the principle that uniting all disabled people was its strength. The founders believed, furthermore, that disabled people must take risks, that is they must dare to succeed. The organization started out small and organized only in Nouakchott, the capital city. It would then grow to have members in all areas of the country.

The organization embarked on employment training projects for disabled persons. In 1978, a work project was set up where ten disabled women were employed making carpets.[24] A year later, a center for training in sewing, embroidery and stenography and typing was started employing disabled people. Organizations such as Oxfam, Caritas, and the Canadian and US embassies helped in providing equipment. The project's aim was to provide disabled people with the skills to be integrated into the regular workforce.

The Union also took the lead in forming a regional network of disabled people's organizations in West Africa, the West African Federation for the Advancement of Handicapped Persons (WAFAH). Goodwill Industries of America facilitated the formation of the network. In 1978, Goodwill decided to co-sponsor a conference in the field of rehabilitation of disabled people in Africa. At the conference, delegates decided they wished to form a permanent network to share ideas on disability, and this network ultimately resulted in a disabled people's regional federation.

Tambo Camara, a wheelchair-user and bio-chemist from Mauritania, and Susan Roche, an employee of Goodwill Industries, helped disabled leaders to find each other. In November, 1980, disabled people's groups from nine French-speaking countries met together – Senegal, Mali, Mauritania, Togo, Niger, Upper Volta (now renamed Burkina Faso), Benin, Guinea-Conakry and Ivory Coast. They formed the West African Federation for the Advancement of the Handicapped (la Fédération Ouest Africaine des Associations pour la Promotion des Personnes Handicapées [WAFAH]). The organization "was conceived of as a membership organization that would bring together both rehabilitation 'professionals' and disabled persons organizations".[25] The distinction between professionals and disabled people was blurred, since many African professionals were disabled themselves. And in addition, many disabled people's organizations, such as the Mauritanian Union, provided services, or would provide rehabilitation and employment services in the future. The constitution, however, did not provide for majority control by disabled people. Tambo Camara travelled to Winnipeg, Canada, in 1980 to the Rehabilitation International World Congress as a representative of the emerging WAFAH, and participated in the founding of DPI.

Joshua Malinga, a crutch-user as a result of polio, also travelled to the Winnipeg World Congress in 1980. He was one of the founders of the self-help organization in Zimbabwe. The National Council of Disabled Persons of Zimbabwe (NCDPZ) had its roots in the Jairos Jiri Association for the Rehabilitation of the Disabled and Blind, which was the biggest rehabilitation center for blacks in what was then white-controlled Rhodesia. It trained disabled people in basket-weaving, leathercraft and shoe-repairing, and it offered some literacy classes.

In the mid-1960s, a disabled people's council was started within the institution.[26] It evolved by 1970 into the Kubatsirana Welfare Society, whose name meant "helping one another".[27] The executives of the Jairos Jiri institution were threatened by the new united voice of disabled people, who were speaking out on issues in the center. But disabled people felt they needed to speak out: "First and foremost disabled persons felt it necessary that they should represent and speak for themselves in all matters that affected them. It was out of natural necessity that such an organization be formed because disabled people were being misunderstood, ignored, misrepresented and exploited."[28]

It took four years for the National Council for the Welfare of the Disabled, as the self-help group renamed itself, to be registered as an organization because the service providers opposed the idea. Jairos Jiri and other agencies called these disabled people radical and ungrateful after all they had done for them. The government thought the new Council was duplicating the work of service-providing organizations. But this opposition served to spur the members of the Council on in their determination to have their own organization controlled by disabled persons. The Council was registered in 1975, but it kept a low profile until 1980 because of the big fight that had ensued over registration.

The Council entered the international arena when Oxfam funded Malinga's participation to the founding meeting of DPI in Winnipeg. Malinga knew that the philosophy he talked about with others from around the world was what was needed for Zimbabwe.[29]

ASIA/PACIFIC

In the 1980s, 250 million disabled people, half the world's total of 500 million, lived in the Asia/Pacific region, which embraced the Middle East, South Asia, South-east Asia and the Far East. Ninety per cent of disabled people were unable to read or write. Eighty per cent lived in rural areas, but they had little access to services because 90 per cent of service and rehabilitation facilities were in the cities.[30] According to the World Health Organization, only 2 per cent of disabled people received any kind of services.[31]

Overall, the birth of a disabled child for a family was an unhappy event:

For millions of families in absolute poverty, the birth of a disabled child (or an illness or accident producing serious impairment) places them in a slightly worse position than their neighbours. It may affect adversely the marriage opportunities of the rest of the family.[32]

Many religions, such as Shinto and Buddhism, viewed disabled people as a curse on the family. They were seen as badges of shame which indicated that the family might have committed some sin in the past.[33] As a result, people with disabilities were often hidden away.

Disabled women in particular had few options or status in the developing world, as Dr Fatima Shah, a visually-impaired woman from Pakistan, explained:

Women in general have power as wives and mothers within the home, and their status in society comes from this role. A disabled woman, in general, cannot share in this status. She is not seen as *marriageable* – no one wants to arrange a marriage with "damaged goods". Also, in the developing world, women perform most of the labor in the home and on the fields. A disabled woman often cannot perform this work as efficiently as a nondisabled woman. Consequently a disabled woman has no status because she cannot accomplish those tasks which bring women status in her society.[34]

Both disabled women and men had few options for employment and meaningful work in these societies. Many disabled people begged in the streets of the big cities, as they did in Africa. Religions called on their followers to give to the needy, sick and disabled to build credit toward an afterlife:

Dropping coins into the blind beggar's bowl may lead to avoidance of punishment in the afterlife. . . . The disabled beggar asks for "justice". Since fate, Karma, or deity has deprived him, begging becomes his rightful duty and occupation: justice demands that his bowl be filled. If the unseen forces present a poor family with a deformed baby, it is the family's duty to exploit the deformity for financial gain.[35]

There were developed countries in the Asia/Pacific region, such as Japan, Australia and Singapore, that did not have an abundance of beggars in the streets.

Before 1980, few countries had self-help organizations which included all disability groups. Many Asian countries such as Singapore and Pakistan had blind organizations associated with the International Federation of the Blind.[36] Ron Chandran-Dudley, a member of the Singapore organisation of the blind, travelled to Winnipeg for the 1980 Rehabilitation International Congress. In Thailand there was an organization of deaf people, and in Fiji an organization of paraplegics. In developed countries like Japan, there were many local and small groups of disabled people, but they were not unified nationally. In Australia, there were local self-help groups that emerged in the 1970s, but they were not very strong and were uni-disability e.g. mentally handicapped people's groups and wheelchair-users' organizations.[37]

THE MIDDLE EAST

In the Middle East, there were organizations of disabled people, of one kind or another, in most countries. There was an umbrella group of people with various disabilities in Israel. In other countries, however, blind persons' organizations were the most common. In Bahrain there was a strong Mobility International group, a travel and recreation organization composed mainly of disabled people. Two of its members, Alice Ma'Louf and Hanan Kamal, attended the 1980 World Congress in Winnipeg.[38]

LATIN AMERICA

In the 1980s, there were 34 million people with various disabilities – physical, mental and sensory – in Latin America (approximately 10 per cent of the population). Most of these were the poorest of the poor.[39]

Many organizations of disabled people were based on Christianity and were formed in nine Latin American countries. These organizations, called Christian 'Fraternities' of disabled people, had originated in France, having been started in 1942 by Monsignor Henri François. The ideas spread to other countries in Europe, and to Central and South America, and organizations sprang up that promoted the abilities and integration of disabled people. These groups included people with all kinds of disabilities, and disabled people were in the majority on their boards.[40] In Brazil, for instance, where the movement started in 1942, there were 200 nuclei, or small groups, in different regions of the country by 1985.[41]

By the late 1970s, secular organizations had been formed in Argentina, Costa Rica, Cuba, El Salvador and Nicaragua for mutual support and for action to correct injustices. Nicaragua founded its organization after Somoza was overthrown in 1979: it started with young disabled war veterans.[42] In Argentina, the Corporación Argentina de Discapacitados (CADIS) began after the polio epidemic of 1956, when individuals disabled as a result of the epidemic formed a social/recreational club. The organization was not initially involved in lobbying for changes in society. The United Nations' sponsored International Year of Disabled Persons, 1981, heightened the world's awareness of the barriers facing disabled people and the need for their integration into society. At this time, the Argentine social club became an organization concerned with rights. Jacqueline de las Carreras, a wheelchair-user as a result of polio and one of their main leaders, attended the founding meeting of DPI in 1980 and met disabled people there who espoused this new rights-oriented philosophy. She brought it back to Argentina.

THE CARIBBEAN

Disabled persons' groups rose against the background of decolonization, and the struggle of countries for independence in the Caribbean. Already in the 1930s, '40s and '50s people were asking for social reforms. The university campuses (especially in Jamaica) were quite radical in the 1960s. People saw that blacks were declaring themselves "beautiful" in the United States, and were waging a civil rights struggle. They tended to view what the United States was doing in Vietnam as imperialism and wondered if they could become another Vietnam. Indeed, the US influence in the region since the 1960s has been great – culturally, economically and militarily – with the presence of US ships and submarines. Against this background young blind students, who met each other in separate schools for the blind, led the way for disabled people's rights, establishing organizations controlled by blind people in the mid-1970s.[43]

It was only in the late 1970s that disabled people of all disability groups began to come together. Jamaica, often viewed as a leader in the Caribbean, became the first country to establish a multi-disability organization.[44] The Combined Disabilities Association Ltd. (CDA) was formally born in 1981. It had a great impact in Jamaica and won greater accessibility to public buildings and to the public education system. In Jamaica, as in other developing countries, disabled people occupied the lowest rung in society. Some 100 social welfare organizations looked after the needs of the "less fortunate", including disabled people. But as the Combined Disabilities Association explained,

Traditionally, they have been conservative and patronizing. As a result, many social welfare projects have been known to perpetuate dependency, more so in the lesser developed ex-colonial societies where programs have been so designed that they inadvertantly limit the potential of the recipients to strive towards self-reliance. This is particularly so among the disabled.[45]

The CDA asserted that disabled people themselves knew which programs met their needs. The CDA was the voice of disabled people, but it would also be open to service provision. "Except where a service is lacking or requires urgent development, the CDA's policy is not to duplicate private or government agencies but to urge and assist them to extend their services to all disabled persons in society."[46]

The developed countries

EUROPE

Blind people and deaf people organized in separate groups in Europe by the late nineteenth century in countries such as Sweden, Denmark and Norway.[47] In Denmark, people with disabilities were organized into uni-disability groups in the late nineteenth and early twentieth centuries, and these groups joined together in 1934.[48] Many organizations of disabled people began after the Second World War to meet the rehabilitation, technical aids and pension needs of persons disabled by the war, polio and workplace accidents.

As mentioned earlier, there was a regional coalition of disabled people's organizations, Fédération Internationale des Mutilés, des Invalides du Travail et des Invalides Civils (FIMITIC) founded in 1953. Most of the European disabled people's groups belonged to this organization.

In Italy people of various disabilities organized the Associazione Nazionale Mutilati ed Invalidi Civili. Its aim was to promote the integration of disabled people.[49] In the Netherlands after the war, disabled people formed uni-disability groups, and by 1977 they united into one organization, the Council of the Dutch Disabled.[50] In the United Kingdom disabled people organized into local uni-disability groups in the mid-1970s. Service and welfare organizations for disabled persons were very strong financially and held a high public profile in Britain, with people receiving titles and honours for their participation in charitable organizations for disabled people. But by November 1981 disabled people had organized themselves into the British Council of Organizations of Disabled People.[51] In West Germany there were two main groups, the disabled war veterans and a civilian group.[52] They were not activist-oriented in their approach to issues – there was little protesting in the streets. They have received many income security and vocational rehabilitation benefits from their government since the Second World War.[53]

In France, the Paralysés de France was founded in 1933. It operated services for disabled people in rehabilitation, technical aids, employment and counselling. It also pressed for disabled people's rights by lobbying the government.[54] In the Soviet Union there existed a blind organization, a group of deaf people, and some organizations of physically disabled people.[55] In Hungary local uni-disability organizations were started in 1977, and by 1981 mobility-impaired people had formed a national federation of local disabled people's groups.[56]

The Swedes, through the visually-impaired Bengt Lindqvist, were to play a major role in the founding of DPI. Indeed, the Swedes had some of the oldest organizations of disabled people in the world. Disabled people in Sweden had been organized in the late nineteenth century, and the movement for their participation in society had begun earlier in the second half of the century. At that time in Sweden popular citizens' movements (the *folkroralser*), trade unionists, the temperance movement and non-conformist or "free church" movements were prevalent,[57] with broad grassroots support. Disabled people learned many lessons from observing other popular movements, and their movement grew amidst this atmosphere of change.

The Stockholm Association for the Deaf was founded in 1868 and the National Association of the Blind in 1889.[58] Throughout the 1920s and '30s, organizations of various disability groups, mainly of mobility-handicapped people, were set up. In 1964 a coalition of uni-disability organizations, Handicappförbundens Centralkommitté (HCK), was born. The HCK promoted integration and rights for disabled people.[59] It received funding from the Swedish Government, which also consulted it on issues of concern to disabled persons:

The movement of disabled has to a large degree been accepted by society's bodies as a consultative partner with regard to the design of measures in the disability sphere. The disabled are given an opportunity to voice their opinion on draft bills, they take part in reference groups, working parties, committees etc., appointed to carry out special investigations at central government, country and municipal levels. They are also in many cases members of permanent bodies, e.g. boards of institutions.[60]

The HCK was also concerned with how disabled people defined themselves in relation to society. The group decided that disabled people were not to blame for their lack of participation, and concluded that the problem lay with a society that excluded disabled persons because it assumed that they could not participate. Thus, society had built physical barriers, stairs and curbs. And it had erected attitudinal barriers that held that people with disabilities were sick and incapable of participation. These views would play an integral role in the philosophy of the new Disabled Peoples' International.

The Swedish organizations of disabled people had one of the longest histories in the world. They also had the support of their government and society in changes to enable their participation in society. They also had influence in the Swedish delegation to the Winnipeg World Congress, where DPI would be initiated. Bengt Lindqvist of the HCK was to be one of the leading players in the new organization.

NORTH AMERICA

In the late 1960s and early 1970s, in the United States, university students with severe disabilities began the "independent living movement". In Berkeley, students at the University of California organized the Center for Independent Living (CIL) in 1972.[61] They did so because the services they needed to live independently in the community, such as attendant care,[62] were not provided after they graduated from university. They banded together with other interested disabled people in the community, most of whom were wheelchair-users. Some blind persons also joined. The Center provided attendant care services, peer counselling and a reading service for blind persons.[63]

The CIL was managed and controlled by persons with disabilities themselves. Up till this point in the United States, services for disabled people were provided and controlled by nondisabled, professional service-givers in institutions, hospitals and rehabilitation centers. The "independent living center" philosophy claimed that:

1. Those who best know the needs of disabled people and how to meet those needs are disabled people themselves. 2. The needs of the disabled can be met

most effectively by comprehensive programs which provide a variety of services
3. Disabled people should be integrated as fully as possible into their community.[64]

Soon after the birth of the CIL, independent living centers began springing up in other parts of the United States on both coasts.[65]

The organizers and users of these centers tended to come mainly from certain disability groups: muscular dystrophy, spinal cord injuries, multiple sclerosis, postpolio disablement and cerebral palsy. The independent living movement itself has focussed on older adolescents and young working adults or students in their twenties.[66] Also this movement grew in university communities, where students were freed from family and economic responsibilities, and thus had more time and energy to organize for change.

Not only were independent living centers spawned in the early 1970s, but a new ''consumer'' movement of disabled people emerged as well. In 1974, the American Coalition of Citizens With Disabilities (ACCD) was formed, bringing together groups such as Disabled in Action of New York, and some independent living centers. Many of the organizations' members met each other during the fight for passage of the Rehabilitation Act, a kind of Bill of Rights for American disabled people.[67] By 1979, the ACCD represented fifty-five groups and spoke for 7 million people with various disabilities.[68] It saw itself as a voice of disabled people, not a service-providing national organization.

The consumerism concept – that disabled people as consumers of services have a right to monitor the quality of those services – became even more pronounced in Canada. There, disabled people organized a national organization in 1976. The Canadian movement sprang up independently of that in the United States; there was no contact between US and Canadian disabled people's groups. But it appeared that the US black civil rights movement, the activities of consumer advocate Ralph Nader, the women's movement and the independent living movement created a climate of change; and new ideas spilled into Canada. Organizations of disabled persons, once again spearheaded by young mobility-impaired people, many of them university students and professionals, had sprung up in all ten Canadian provinces by 1979. These organizations united into the Coalition of Provincial Organizations of the Handicapped (COPOH) in 1976. This organization was the only national multi-disability organization in Canada, and purported to represent the interests of people of all disabilities. It lobbied the federal government for the protection of disabled people in the Canadian Human Rights Act.[69]

COPOH did not provide any services for disabled people, such as attendant care, counselling or transportation. It was a voice requesting that the federal and provincial governments provide accessible services to disabled people, just as they would to all other citizens. Canada was a welfare state in that it provided subsidized medical care for all, and mobility aids such as wheelchairs and crutches to people who could not afford them. Thus, for example, disabled people expected the government to provide for attendant care services in the community for persons who wanted them. This approach was somewhat different from in the United States, where there was neither a universal health care system nor an expectation that government would look after all one's health and personal physical care needs.

COPOH and the HCK, its Swedish counterpart, assisted by American disabled activists, were to play important roles as catalysts for the beginnings of DPI. They would unite disabled people from different regions around the common goal of wanting their own voice. The beginnings of DPI were to take place at the 1980 World Congress of Rehabilitation International (RI) in Winnipeg, Canada, where COPOH had its head office.

NOTES

1   Ed Roberts, "When others speak for you, you lose" in Jeff Heath (*ed.*), *'When Others Speak for You, You Lose,' Proceedings of the First National Assembly of Disabled Peoples' International (Australia), Melbourne, Jan. 1983* (Adelaide: South Australian Chapter of DPI, 1984).

2   Irving Kenneth Zola, "Helping One Another: A Speculative History of the Self-Help Movement", *Archives of Physical and Medical Rehabilitation* 60 (Oct. 1979), 453; Diane Driedger, "The Struggle for Legitimacy: A History of the Coalition of Provincial Organizations of the Handicapped (COPOH)" in Aileen Wight-Felske (*ed.*) *Dialogue on Disability*: vol. II (Calgary: University of Calgary Press, forthcoming), 2.

3   Health and Welfare Canada, *Disabled Persons in Canada* (Ottawa: Minister of Supply and Services Canada, 1980), 21.

4   *Ibid.*

5   Henry Enns, "The Historical Development of Attitudes Toward the Handicapped: A Framework for Change" in David S. Freeman and Barry Trute (*eds*), *Treating Families With Special Needs* (Ottawa: Canadian Association of Social Workers, 1981), 178–9.

6   Derksen, *The Disabled Consumer Movement*, 5.

7   These organizations were formed throughout the 1950s, '60s and early '70s. The following are examples. Epilepsy International was incorporated in 1977, and was a

union of two world organizations – the International League Against Epilepsy, and the International Bureau for Epilepsy (Epilepsy International, "Comprehensive Planning for Epilepsy 1982–1986", 1982, document in author's possession, hereafter signified by an asterisk [*]). The International Cerebral Palsy Society was founded in 1969 (Anita Loring, Secretary General, International Cerebral Palsy Society, to Diane Driedger, Mar. 1, 1985*). The International League of Societies for Persons with Mental Handicap (ILSMH) was formed in 1960 by representatives of small national parents' groups (ILSMH, *What is the International League of Societies for Persons With Mental Handicap [ILSMH]?* [Brussels: ILSMH, 1984]*). The International Ostomy Association was formed in 1975. (Edwin J. Ward, "A Message From Edwin J. Ward: The International Ostomy History", *International Ostomy Association Bulletin*, Spring 1980). The World Federation of Hemophilia (WFH) was founded in 1963 (WFH, "Information Sheet", Sept. 1984, 1*). The World Council for the Welfare of the Blind (WCWB), founded in 1951, was formed for providing services for blind people in seventy-seven countries. The World Federation for Mental Health was founded in 1948 in London ("What is WFMH?", pamphlet, undated). As of 1982 the World Rehabilitation Association for the Psycho-Socially Disabled was in formation. (*International Psychiatric Rehabilitation Newsletter* 2 [May–June 1982]).

8   Council of World Organizations Interested in the Handicapped, *CWOIH Compendium, 1981* (New York: Rehabilitation International, 1981), 1–111.

9   World Federation of the Deaf, "The World Federation of the Deaf in the Eighties" (pamphlet), *ca.* 1984.*

10   CWOIH, *CWOIH Compendium*, 45–6.

11   Arne Husveg, "World Blind Union Founded – A Victory for Solidarity and Good Sense", *Vox Nostra* 2 (Feb. 1984), 18.

12   Interview with Dr Fatima Shah, DPI World Council member, Kingston, Jamaica, Sept. 28, 1984.

13   *Ibid.*

14   *Ibid.*

15   *Ibid.*

16   Interview with Bengt Lindqvist, DPI honorary secretary, Nassau, Bahamas, Sept. 21, 1985; John Colligan, "WCWB" in *The New Beacon* (Mar. 1985), 83; World Blind Union, "Brief Presentation", Mar. 1985.*

17   Jean Parker Edwards, *We Are People First: Our handicaps are secondary* (Portland, Oregon: EDNICK, 1982), 16.

18   Serigne Bamba N'Diaye, "Evaluation du programme de développement séminaires africains de Dakar et Nouakchott", 1985, 6, DPI Development Office files, Winnipeg.

19   Robin Morgan and Gloria Steinem, "The Crime of Genital Mutilation" in Gloria Steinem, *Outrageous Acts and Everyday Rebellions* (New York: Holt, Rinehart, Winston, 1983), 292–300; Swedish International Development Authority, *The Women's Dimension in Development Assistance: SIDA's Plan of Action* (Stockholm: SIDA Office of Women in Development, 1985), 16.

20   N'Diaye, "*Evaluation*", 5–6.

21   *Ibid.*, 7.

22   *Ibid.*, 16.

23   *Ibid.*, 16–17.

24 Tambo Camara, DPI vice chairperson for Africa, to Diane Driedger, April 28, 1985, 3.*

25 Robert Ransom, director, International Department, Goodwill Industries of America, to Diane Driedger, July 31, 1985, p. 2.*

26 Interview with Joshua Malinga, DPI honorary treasurer, Kingston, Jamaica, Sept. 30, 1984.

27 National Council of Disabled Persons in Zimbabwe, "The Organization of all Disabled Zimbabweans" (pamphlet), *ca.* 1984.*

28 National Council of Disabled Persons of Zimbabwe, "A Voice of Our Own", Bulawayo, April 1983, 1, DPI Development Office files, Winnipeg.

29 Malinga interview.

30 DPI Asia/Pacific, "Leadership Training Seminar Asia/Pacific Regional Council Disabled Peoples' International", 2, DPI Development Office files, Winnipeg.

31 Economic and Social Commission for Asia and the Pacific (ESCAP), "Economic and Social Commission for Asia and the Pacific Regional Program on Disability Concerns", no date, 2, DPI Development Office files, Winnipeg.

32 Mike Miles, "Why Asia Rejects Western Disability Advice", *Quad Wrangle* 6 (Dec. 1983), 27.

33 Aki Ninomiya, DPI Japan, "Disabled People in Japan", address, Winnipeg, Aug. 17, 1984, DPI Development Office files, Winnipeg.

34 Diane Driedger and April D'Aubin, "Disabled Women: International Profiles ", *Caliper* XLI (March 1986), 16.

35 Miles, "Why Asia Rejects", 27.

36 Driedger and D'Aubin, "Disabled Women", 16.

37 Frank Stevens, "The Self-Help Movement" in Disability Resources Centre (*ed.*), *Into the Streets: A book by and for disabled people* (Collingwood, Australia: Disability Resources Centre, 1981), 11–18.

38 "Roof Association of Organizations of Persons with Disabilities" *ca.* 1981, DPI Development Office files, Winnipeg; Dr Y. Qaryouti, "Middle East Training Program for Leadership of Disabled Persons, First Draft", 1984, DPI Development Office files, Winnipeg; Alice John Ma'louf and Hanan Kamal, "Message", in *Disabled Peoples' International 1st World Congress Souvenir Program*, 13, DPI Development Office files, Winnipeg.

39 João Ferreira, DPI regional vice chairperson, Latin America, "Regional Report of Latin America for the World Council", 1982, DPI Development Office files, Winnipeg.

40 Fraternidade Crista de Doentes e Deficientes (FCD), "Fraternidade Crista de Doentes e Deficientes (FCD)" (pamphlet), Brazil, 1981.*

41 Celso Zoppi, Fraternidade Crista de Doentes e Deficientes (FCD), Brazil, to Diane Driedger, April 28, 1986. 1.*

42 Interview with Freddy Trejos Jarquin, secretary of Organization of Disabled Revolutionaries (ORD), Winnipeg, Nov. 25, 1985.

43 Interview with Derrick Palmer, DPI regional development officer for the Caribbean, Winnipeg, April 22, 1986.

44 *Ibid.*

45 Combined Disabilities Association, "Activity III", *ca.* 1983, DPI, Development Office files, Winnipeg.

46 *Ibid.*, 3.

47   Rolf Utberg to Diane Driedger, *ca.* Jan. 1987*; Yerker Andersson, "Organizations of the Deaf in Developing Countries and Their Relationship to the World Federation of the Deaf", plenary lecture at X World Congress, World Federation of the Deaf, Helsinki, July 27, 1987, 1–2.

48   H. Kallehauge, Danish Anti-Polio Society, to Diane Driedger, *ca.* Oct. 1986.*

49   Associazione Nazionale Mutilati ed Invalidi Civili, "Information Sheet", no date.*

50   Council of the Dutch Disabled, "Council of the Dutch Disabled", Amsterdam, Sept. 1980.*

51   British Council of Organizations of Disabled People, "British Council of Organizations of Disabled People" (pamphlet), London, *ca.* 1986.*

52   Interview with Henry Enns, DPI chairperson, Winnipeg, Canada, July 4, 1985.

53   Hans-Ulrich Greffrath, "The VDK of Germany: Facts and Figures", *ca.* 1986; interview with Jim Derksen, former DPI Chief Development Officer, June 15, 1986; *Bundesverbandes für Spastisch, Gelähmte und andere Körperbehinderte e.V., Das Band* (May 1979).

54   Association des Paralysés de France, *Faire face* (Aug. 1983); Jean Courbeyre, *1933–1983, Le Parcours de l'Association des Paralysés de France: Cinquante Ans de Créations au Service des Personnes Handicapés* (Paris: Association des Paralysés de France, 1983).

55   "Disabled in the USSR – 'a Miserable Existence' ", *Handicaps Monthly,* 136 (Feb. 1982), 47.

56   National Federation of Associations of Disabled Persons, "Disabled People in Hungary", Budapest, *ca.* 1987, 1.

57   Interview with Bengt Lindqvist, DPI honorary secretary, Kingston, Sept. 26, 1984; Barbro and Folke Carlsson, *Social Welfare and Handicap Policy in Sweden* (Stockholm: The Swedish Institute, *ca.* 1981), 26; Linnéa Gardeström, "Handicap Councils: A Swedish Experiment" in Kathleen S. Miller, Linda M. Chadderdon and Barbara Duncan (*eds*), *Participation of People with Disabilities: An International Perspective* (East Lansing, Michigan: University Center for International Rehabilitation, Michigan State University, 1981), 62.

58   Linnéa Gardeström, "The Swedish Handicap Movement", *Current Sweden* 7 (Nov. 1978), 1.

59   The National Council for the Disabled, *Associations and Societies of Disabled in Sweden Directory* (Stockholm: National Council for the Disabled, 1984), 34.

60   The Swedish Institute, *Support for the Disabled in Sweden* (Stockholm: Swedish Institute, 1981), 1.

61   Hale Zukas, "CIL History" (Berkeley, Calif., 1976), 3–4.*

62   "Attendant care" refers to the hiring of a nondisabled person to look after a disabled person's personal needs – such as dressing, bathing, and transferring in and out of bed.

63   Zukas, "CIL History", 3.

64   *Ibid.,* 3.

65   Gerben DeJong, "Independent Living: From Social Movement to Analytic Paradigm", *Archives of Physical Medicine and Rehabilitation* 60 (Oct. 1979), 437.

66   *Ibid.,* 435–6.

67   Terrence O'Rourke, "Coalition Building in the Handicapped Community" in

Jim Derksen (*ed.*), *Report on An Open National Employment Conference, COPOH* (Winnipeg: COPOH, 1979), 49.

68   Sonny Kleinfeld, *The Hidden Minority: A Profile of Handicapped Americans* (Boston: Little, Brown, 1979), 35.

69   Diane Driedger, ''The Struggle for Legitimacy: A History of the Coalition of Provincial Organizations of the Handicapped (COPOH)'' in Aileen Wight-Felske (*ed.*), *Dialogue on Disability*, vol. II (Calgary: University of Calgary Press, forthcoming).

3

RELEASE FROM THE YOKE OF PATERNALISM AND "CHARITY", 1972–1980

"A significant movement becomes possible when there is a revision in the manner in which a substantial group of people, looking at some misfortune, sees it no longer as a misfortune warranting charitable consideration but as an injustice which is intolerable to society."[1]

— Ralph H. Turner, sociologist

"If we have learned one thing from the civil rights movement in the United States it's that when others speak for you, you lose."[2]

— Ed Roberts, 1983

In 1980 disabled people asked for the last time for an equal say in decision-making in Rehabilitation International (RI), an organization of professionals. They broke with RI after being turned down once again. Indeed, disabled people, most of them professionals, were denied an equal voice in RI throughout the 1970s. They had asked to be party to decisions about policies that affected the lives of disabled people around the world. The 1980 RI World Congress in Winnipeg was the watershed of RI's past denials – disabled people took control of their own destiny and Disabled Peoples' International was initiated.

Rehabilitation International and disabled people's participation

Rehabilitation International was an international organization composed mainly of rehabilitation professionals – doctors, physiotherapists, nurses and social workers. It was also the only international organization that addressed the needs of people with various disabilities. RI was founded in 1922 as the "International Society for Crippled Children". Ultimately it changed its mandate to include adults, and changed its name.[3] But this organization tended to view disabled people as sick and childlike patients who needed professionals to care for them from cradle to grave.

RI held World Congresses every four years to discuss rehabilitation and social issues as they related to disabled people, and they were attended by professionals from around the world. Even though the discussion concerned the lives of persons with disabilities, very few disabled people ever participated as speakers, delegates or observers. There were several reasons for their lack of participation. One was a lack of resources. Disabled people, even in the developed Western world, were some of the poorest people in their societies, often depending solely on a small disability pension or begging to support themselves. Since many disabled people were unemployed, they could not afford such a trip, and had no charitable organization or service agency to help them with the costs. These agencies did not view disabled people as experts of any kind, so the amount of funding available was minimal. Able-bodied professionals were assumed to be the experts, while disabled people were thought to be incapable of contributing anything.

Thus, RI had few disabled people participating in their Congresses until the 1970s. In 1972, a few disabled people participated as observers at the Congress, in Sydney, Australia, and they gathered together for discussions.[4] They probably exchanged information about the issues of the Congress and the accessibility of the site, as there were complaints about accessibility for people with disabilities.[5]

At the next World Congress in Tel Aviv, Israel, in 1976, a greater number of disabled people were present. Although they were still only a handful amidst 800 delegates, they made a militant stand. They met separately at the Congress and complained about the inaccessibility of the Congress site and their accommodation. There were also transportation problems. People with disabilities were loaded up into military vehicles and driven around. They felt that this was very humiliating and believed that RI, an organization purporting to speak and act on behalf of disabled persons, showed inconsistency because it did not even think it important enough to have accessible facilities.[6] The disabled people there concluded that in the long term it would not benefit disabled people in general to be a part of RI.[7]

From the point of view of the RI World Congress organizers, the Tel Aviv Congress had been organized in a hurry due to unforeseen difficulties. Originally, it had been planned to take place in the German Democratic Republic (East Germany), and was then transferred to Poland. Ultimately, because of political troubles in Poland, it was transferred to Tel Aviv. As a result, according to Norman Acton, Secretary General of RI at the time, "Because of the shortness of time, it was necessary to improvise in many ways on both the program and the physical facilities for the Congress. One special difficulty had to do with the movement of people with mobility problems between various meeting sites, and there were other access snags."[8]

However, the disabled people present felt that their needs had been ignored, not only in Israel, but at previous World Congresses. They wanted physical access to RI Congresses. After all, if they could not enter the meeting site, how could they participate? At the closing plenary session of the Congress, Liam Maguire, a wheelchair-user from Ireland, spoke passionately about the accessibility problems. As Ron Chandran-Dudley, of Singapore recalled: "[He let] the participants present and the world know that merely talking about disabled people and their problems was not good enough. We needed action, accesibility and equality. We were also human beings."[9] Furthermore, as a Swedish delegate, Linnéa Gardeström, related: "It was a plenary session and he complained very much about the bad accessibility which he thought showed that the disabled themselves were not welcomed at the meeting . . . I remember his speech mostly as a very impressive protest against the arrangements . . ."[10]

For the first time, many people within RI became aware of the frustration of disabled people, who had the expectation that they should be treated as equal to service providers at international meetings that addressed the needs of disabled people. They had increased physical mobility, due to technological advances, education and the experience of being disabled, and they believed that they should be included in the planning process. Thus, the meetings needed to be physically accessible to them.

Ultimately, probably in large part due to the frustration of disabled people, RI decided at its Delegate Assembly (or board) meeting at Baguio, in the Philippines, in January 1978 to begin looking at the issue of disabled people's participation in RI. An Ad Hoc Committee on the Participation of Disabled People was set up for this purpose.

Throughout 1978 and 1979, the Ad Hoc Committee discussed a draft resolution to be presented at the next Delegate Assembly of RI at Winnipeg, Canada, in June 1980. The Draft Resolution recognized that ". . . in many countries increased organizational activity by persons with disabilities is taking place and is influencing the planning and provision of rehabilitation services. . . ."[11]

Furthermore, it affirmed that it should be the policy of Rehabilitation International to:

a. Require and assist the full participation in Rehabilitation International of organizations of disabled people. *b*. Provide that, after 1984, a requirement for membership in Rehabilitation International shall be that each member organization has adopted a policy of requiring and assisting the full participation in its governance of organizations of disabled people. *c*. Urge present member organizations to adopt as soon as possible and no later than 1988 the policy stated in the previous paragraph. *d*. Continue to actively encourage the participation of persons with disabilities at all levels in Rehabilitation International's governing bodies.[12]

While RI was addressing the participation problem, members of the RI Delegate Assembly in Sweden were discussing the same matter. In most countries, the several organizations that provided services for disabled people belonged to RI. In Sweden, however, the HCK – the coalition of various organizations of disabled people – and not just nondisabled professionals belonged to RI. In Sweden, the HCK had input into choosing the Swedish delegation to RI's decision-making Delegate Assembly, and in the end the delegation was composed of four representatives of whom at least two were people with disabilities themselves. Thus, this delegation very much represented the concerns of organizations of disabled people.

The Swedish delegation drafted a proposal for equal representation of disabled people's organizations on national delegations to the Assembly.[13] Under this proposal disabled people's organizations would have an equal say in decision-making. The Swedish disabled people expected that disabled people should have the same decision-making power over economic resources and social policies in RI as nondisabled professionals. Their proposal for equal representation arose out of their belief that, compared to nondisabled professionals, disabled people had little say about policies dealing directly with their own concerns. This was just what some of the other disabled people's groups were thinking.

The threat of Canadian non-cooperation

The Coalition of Provincial Organizations of the Handicapped (COPOH), the national organization of disabled people in Canada, also planned a strategy for disabled people's participation in Rehabilitation International for the upcoming World Congress in Winnipeg, its headquarters. COPOH wanted to drive home the principle that disabled people were partners in planning services, and it wanted the public and professionals to recognize that it had a right to an equal say in decisions about disabled people's lives. COPOH made a bid for RI membership, and for this the Canadian Rehabilitation Council for the Disabled (CRCD), an organization of rehabilitation professionals and already an RI member, would have to give its consent. The negotiation process about membership between COPOH and CRCD was fraught with conflict and tension.

COPOH warned that it would protest outside the doors of the Congress if CRCD did not accept its membership. Thus, in the end, the Canadian government, through its Rehabilitation Bureau, helped to mediate the discussions; it was contributing funding towards the hosting of the World Congress in Winnipeg, and was concerned that everything should go well. It had heard of disabled people's protests at the previous World Congress in Tel Aviv, and did not want an international incident at this event, which the media would be covering.[14]

Ultimately, CRCD supported COPOH's membership. This signalled a victory for COPOH, who viewed this as recognition that it was a partner with professionals in planning about disabled people's lives. It was also agreed, since COPOH wished to participate in the Congress in some way, that two of COPOH's leaders, Chairperson Allan Simpson and National Coordinator Jim Derksen, both wheelchair-users, would prepare papers on the disabled people's movement for the Congress. And COPOH agreed to help with planning transportation and accommodation for disabled delegates to the Congress. COPOH also received a grant from the Health and Welfare Department of the Canadian Government to bring fifty Canadian disabled delegates to Winnipeg.[15]

A world organization established in Winnipeg

COPOH geared up for the Congress in Winnipeg by arranging for its fifty delegates to arrive early, before the formal opening of the Congress. It had at its disposal several important resources which it mobilized for action: monitoring, strategies and tactics, and media coverage. It worked out a strategy on how to have input into the RI Congress, which would be attended predominantly by 3,000 nondisabled professionals. The approach was threefold.

First, it would make contact with the media and alert them to COPOH's intention to monitor the attitudes reflected in Congress papers and sessions. Secondly, COPOH delegates would monitor each day's activities and record them on a form that COPOH had drawn up for this purpose. The monitoring sheets would be submitted by COPOH delegates at the end of the day, and COPOH staff would then put together a daily newsheet to be circulated around the Congress. Thirdly, COPOH would facilitate and organize information-sharing sessions among disabled delegates from around the world. To do all this COPOH needed an on-site secretariat. Luckily, an agency called "Concept", an employment training program run for and by disabled people, had its office in the building where the Congress was to take place. Concept offered COPOH space at the front of its office for a secretariat during the Congress.

The fifty COPOH delegates arrived in Winnipeg three days before the actual Congress, and met for strategy training sessions. The COPOH "Parameters of Rehabilitation Open National Forum", held a few months earlier in Vancouver, helped COPOH members to develop policies for input into the RI World Congress. COPOH believed that rehabilitation stopped after a person reached his/her maximum capacity, and that independent living for the person began after this point. After all, disabled people did not wish to remain for ever the "sick patients" of medical experts and the "caseloads" of social workers. Media coverage began during the planning sessions. The Canadian Broadcasting Corporation's (CBC) "Summerscope" television program began filming COPOH before the Congress and followed the disabled delegates around all week.[16]

RI held its Delegate Assembly meeting on Friday and Saturday, June 20–21, just before the beginning of the Congress. The Ad Hoc Committee on the Participation of Disabled People and Their Organizations presented its draft resolution. Then the visually-impaired Bengt Linqvist, member of the Swedish delegation, introduced the Swedish draft resolution. It was submitted as an amendment to the RI draft resolution and called for a definition of organizations of disabled people and required such organizations to have at least 50 per cent of the delegates in any national delegation. In other words, half of the Delegate Assembly should be composed of disabled people.

The amendment was defeated 61–37.[17] This defeat was a result of feelings on the part of RI delegates that a rigid quota for disabled people's involvement should not be imposed. In their view, election to positions should be based on people's qualifications, and furthermore, some RI delegates believed that RI should reflect all interests – professional, government and disabled people's organizations – in its organization.

Within that framework, they could then give increased attention to disabled people's participation in the future.[18]

The Swedish delegation was angered by the amendment's defeat. It believed that the RI draft resolution, which was passed without the Swedish amendment, was just words. The resolution had no power to force RI members to include disabled people in decision-making. Disabled people wanted to have equal input with professionals immediately, not in the future. Indeed, many disabled people, themselves professionals in social work and other rehabilitation disciplines, attended this Congress for the first time in significant numbers. They were proving that disabled people could indeed work and contribute to society like all so-called normal people. They were no longer in need of rehabilitation. They wanted to speak for themselves about how services could better be delivered to maximize their independence in the community. Their rising expectations had been frustrated by RI.

About 250 individuals with various disabilities attended the Congress. Many of them were American professionals who were disabled. Some of them, and those from other countries, had been invited to participate in the program of the Congress, such as Derksen and Simpson of COPOH and Ed Roberts, one of the founders of the independent living movement in California, and the Director of Rehabilitation for the State of California.[19] RI had invited these people in order to increase the participation of people with disabilities.

Other disabled people, especially from North America, had the money to pay their own way because they had professional jobs. In addition, COPOH had fifty of its own delegates funded by the Canadian government. And because the United Nations International Year of Disabled Persons, 1981, was fast approaching, some individuals with disabilities (particularly from developing countries) received funding from non-governmental organizations to attend.[20] Most of them represented organizations of disabled people in their countries. COPOH facilitated communication among the disabled people from forty countries attending the Congress.

COPOH recruited a taxi cab driver to deliver the daily COPOH *Newsline*, evaluating the events of the Congress, to the thirty hotels where Congress delegates were housed. The *Newsline* was also placed on the desks of reporters in the media room every morning, thus ensuring media coverage of the disabled people's struggle to be heard. The local RI Congress organizers became aware that this *Newsline* was becoming very popular and causing commotion. One morning, some of them went to the media room and collected all the copies of the *Newsline* from the desks before the reporters came in. One reporter caught them at it, and told them to leave the *Newsline* alone, because "that was the only interesting thing happening at this Congress."[21] The *Newsline* also furthered communication among international disabled delegates and COPOH, as it announced separate information-sharing meetings that COPOH hosted outside Congress hours.

COPOH sponsored an interfaith seminar and church service for international delegates to share experiences on the Sunday preceding the Congress, June 22, 1980. This event was well attended, and international disabled delegates displayed an interest in sharing with Canadian disabled people. Thus, COPOH decided to call an information-sharing meeting for disabled people on the first night of the Congress, June 23. The Swedes, angered at their resolution's defeat, swept into the June 23 information-sharing meeting. There 250 disabled people from forty countries learned from Bengt Lindqvist that RI had defeated the equality amendment, and a bond was immediately created among the participants. The group decided that there was a need for an autonomous organization of disabled persons, as Henry Enns and Allan Simpson of Canada recalled:

A tremendous roar filled the Convention Centre in Winnipeg, Canada, that Monday evening June 23, 1980. The question was repeated, 'Do I hear you say you want a World Coalition of Citizens with Disabilities?' The unanimous response came back, echoing to every corner of the World Congress of Rehabilitation – 'Yes!' The some three hundred [*sic*] delegates who gathered there from all parts of the globe had a sense of their own destiny. They wanted to proclaim their rights, as citizens, to an equal voice in the decision-making of services, the policies and programs that affected them. They were no longer willing to passively accept the control of rehabilitation professionals over their lives. They demanded dignity, equality and full participation in society. They demanded release from the yoke of paternalism and charity . . . [22]

An Ad Hoc Planning Committee was set up to discuss the philosophy, organization and structure for a world organization.[23] Representatives of Canada, Costa Rica, India, Japan, Sweden and Zimbabwe made up the Committee, which met several times over the next few days. The Committee presented its findings at the next meeting of disabled delegates on June 25. The group accepted its proposal for a structure and philosophy for starting up an international organization. A Steering Committee was struck with two representatives from seven regions of the world.[24] Henry Enns, a Canadian wheelchair-user, was elected chairperson, and Bengt Lindqvist of Sweden was chosen as vice-chairperson. The organization was struck in great excitement, as a declaration of independence from the control of rehabilitation professionals.

The new organization's name was the World Coalition of Persons with Disabilities (WCPD); it was renamed Disabled Peoples' International (DPI) in the coming months. The organization would be composed entirely of people with disabilities. Its philosophy was equality and justice: "The World Coalition of Persons With Disabilities should be based on the philosophy of equal opportunity and full participation of handicapped people in all aspects of society as a matter of justice rather than charity."[25] The organization was to be multi-disability, that is, organizations of persons of various disabilities would be members. Furthermore the organization's philosophy was one of "self-representation": "The coalition should be firmly committed to the principle that handicapped people are their own best spokespersons. Therefore, the organization should be made up of organizations 'of' the handicapped rather than 'for' the handicapped."[26]

The Steering Committee was mandated to draft a constitution for the new organization, to plan a first world congress to found the organization, and to build organizations of disabled people around the world.[27] Finally, the gathering recognized RI's contribution to the new world voice: "We compliment Rehabilitation International for making possible the vehicle for the formulation of the world coalition."[28]

There were different reactions to the formation of this breakaway group at the RI Congress. One group was incredulous. They were mainly nondisabled professionals, who believed that disabled people would not be able to form their own world organization.[29] These professionals tended to patronize disabled people and this was perhaps one of the reasons why the equal participation resolution was defeated. They believed that disabled people were not ready to speak out for themselves. Ed Roberts, the quadraplegic director of the Department of Rehabilitation in California, claimed that several of these people had even patted him on the head.[30]

The patronizing attitude of professionals reflected their traditional medical model view that disabled people were patients to be cured. As Linnéa Gardeström, a member of the Swedish delegation observed: "Doctors and others working for disabled persons as patients just could not understand why disabled people were not unsatisfied. They looked upon disabled people as weak and in need of assistance from the experts. The rehabilitation professionals had always done their best, why were not disabled people grateful?"[31] But disabled persons were redefining their situation in the world, and they asserted that they were not helpless, passive patients. Rather, they were citizens with rights. Disabled people wanted to represent themselves, for, as Jim Derksen, COPOH National Coordinator, told the media: "Rehabilitation International is a service organization concerned with services, not rights. They don't have the direct experience [of being disabled]."[32]

Some rehabilitation professionals present agreed that disabled people should form their own organization to represent themselves. Rehabilitation International had arranged for more disabled people to participate in the Winnipeg Congress than ever before. They had been granted places on the program. RI anticipated and welcomed the possibility that disabled people would get together at the Congress. However, some rehabilitation people believed that disabled people were going through a phase, but this was something more positive than negative. Archie Carmichael of the Society for Crippled Children and Adults of Manitoba summed up this view:

Most of these people have gone through our "process" and many have been very successful vocationally and/or socially. After all, the purpose of rehabilitation programs is to attain maximum independence. Consumer groups can do many things other programs cannot do. These groups and organizations are new and have not as yet had the benefits of long experience. To me, they are going through a developmental stage which resembles the adolescent or young adult in a family, who often becomes rebellious for a period of time. After this stage, an excellent partnership and relationship with the 'family' evolves and life goes on better than ever.[33]

This was not the view of the disabled people who left Winnipeg and started organizing the new world organization. Indeed, they would be patronized no longer. They were not children as some professionals viewed them – they were adults who were taking control of their lives and destiny as they should. They declared power over their own lives that they believed should have been given to them.

Disabled persons had to wrest power from those with the money and technical resources who would not grant them control. These resources in most countries were controlled either by government or by charitable fund-raising events such as telethons. This form of fund-raising capitalized on the stereotypes the public held about disabled people as pitiful and helpless. The public was moved to contribute money out of guilt and also out of fear that they might catch a disabling condition: thus these conditions needed to be cured before that could happen to them. Most often, cute "crippled" poster children were used to elicit pity. This reinforced the stereotype that disabled persons were perpetual children who needed to be cared for and to be given handouts. Indeed, the World Coalition Steering Committee began its struggle to raise money to organize. Without resources, disabled people could not meet internationally or hold a world congress of their own to launch Disabled Peoples' International.

NOTES

1   Ralph H. Turner, "The theme of contemporary social movements", *British Journal of Sociology* (Dec. 1969), 391.

2   Ed Roberts, "When others speak for you, you lose", in Jeff Heath (*ed.*), *'When Others Speak for You, You Lose', Proceedings of the First National Assembly of Disabled Peoples' International (Australia)*, Melbourne Jan. 1983 (Adelaide: South Australian Chapter of DPI, 1984).

3   Rehabilitation International, "Rehabilitation International: 60 Years as a World Organization", *International Rehabilitation Review*, first quarter 1982, 1.

4   Norman Acton, former Rehabilitation International secretary general, to Diane Driedger, Aug. 22, 1985, 2.

5   *Ibid.*

6   Interview with Henry Enns, DPI chairperson, about Liam Maguire's views on the Tel Aviv World Congress, Winnipeg, Nov. 20, 1985.

7   Interview with Ed Roberts, vice chairperson, DPI North American Region, on Liam Maguire's views on the Tel Aviv World Congress, Nassau, Bahamas, Sept. 18, 1985.

8   Acton to Driedger, 3.

9   Ron Chandran-Dudley, "Tribute to Liam Maguire", *Disabled Peoples' International Anniversary Journal* (Singapore: the Author, 1984), 55.

10 Linnéa Gardeström, Sweden, to Diane Driedger, Aug. 27, 1985, 1.

11 Rehabilitation International, "Participation of Disabled Persons in Rehabilitation International Draft Resolution, Agenda Item 10a, Annex XII, June 20–21, 1980, Winnipeg.*

12 *Ibid.*

13 Interview with Bengt Lindqvist, hon. secretary, DPI (1981–5), Kingston, Jamaica, Sept. 26, 1984.

14 Interview with Allan Simpson, former national chairperson, COPOH, Winnipeg, Feb. 18, 1984.

15 Telephone interview with André LeBlanc, former director, Bureau on Rehabilitation, Health and Welfare Canada, Ottawa, May 7, 1985.

16 Interview with Jim Derksen, former national coordinator, COPOH, Winnipeg, Feb. 18, 1984.

17 Lindqvist interview; Rehabilitation International, "Report of the Meeting of the Assembly, Winnipeg, Manitoba, Canada, June 20–21, 1980", 6–7.*

18 Acton to Driedger, 3.

19 Roberts interview; Acton to Driedger, 4; "A Summary of Proceedings, ACCD, RIUSA, Rehabilitation International Exploratory Meeting", Washington DC, May 1, 1978, 2, COPOH files, Winnipeg.

20 Telephone interview with André LeBlanc, former director Bureau on Rehabilitation, Dept. of Health and Welfare, Canada, Ottawa, June 10, 1985; Interview with Joshua Malinga, DPI honorary treasurer, Kingston, Sept. 30, 1984.

21 Derksen interview, Feb. 18, 1984.

22 Henry Enns and Allan Simpson, "Decade of Destiny of and for Handicapped People", 1980, DPI Development Office files, Winnipeg.

23 *Ibid.*

24 World Coalition of Persons with Disabilities, "Minutes of Meeting by Steering Committee 1980–06–26, Winnipeg, Canada", 1, DPI Development Office files, Winnipeg.

25 Kathleen S. Miller, "Disabled People Coming Together Internationally", in Kathleen Miller, Linda M. Chadderdon and Barbara Duncan (*eds*), *Participation of People with Disabilities: An International Perspective* (Michigan: University Centre for International Rehabilitation, Michigan State University, 1981), 149.

26 *Ibid.*, 149–50.

27 *Ibid.*, 151.

28 "Report of Ad Hoc Committee for World Coalition of the Disabled", June 25, 1980, 2, DPI Development Office files, Winnipeg.

29 Roberts interview.

30 *Ibid.*

31 Linnéa Gardeström, member of Swedish RI delegation to Winnipeg, 1980, to Diane Driedger, April 4, 1985, 1.*

32 Laurie Streich, "International coalition created by handicapped", *Winnipeg Free Press*, June 26, 1980.

33 J.A. Carmichael, executive director, Society for Crippled Children and Adults of Manitoba, to Rev. Harold H. Wilke, July 21, 1980, Society for Manitobans with Disabilities (formerly Society for Crippled Children and Adults of Manitoba) files, Winnipeg.

4

LAYING A FOUNDATION, 1980–1981

"We believe we can pull off a worldwide coalition to help disabled people. We've already done what people thought impossible. And we've done it in about six months."[1]

— Ed Roberts, February 1981

The Steering Committee to establish DPI met three times throughout 1980 and 1981 to prepare a constitution, to draft a statement of philosophy and to organize a founding world congress. The Steering Committee consisted of eleven members after the RI World Congress, but three vacancies on it remained – one each from Latin America, Asia and Oceania. Two of the vacancies were filled over the next half-year.

The Steering Committee members were of varied backgrounds and disabilities and a few had had experience in international organizations through RI and the International Federation of the Blind. Others had years of experience with national organizations of disabled people. Most of the members were professionals in various fields, their ages ranging generally between thirty-five and forty-seven years.

The DPI Steering Committee members were elected because they were seen by the other disabled people at the RI Congress as representing their interests, and to some extent they were charismatic leaders who were needed at this stage of DPI's development[2] – leaders who could be trusted and who would set a direction for the membership. The leadership was from what would be called the middle classes of society, which is typical of many social movements. Also typical was the fact that it tended to be from the professions.[3]

Steering committee meetings

Henry Enns, a representative of North America, and Chairperson of the Steering Committee, made the initial contacts with the UN and the Canadian International Development Agency (CIDA) to raise funds for the Founding Congress of DPI. Enns, a wheelchair-user as a result of arthritis, had been involved with self-help organizations in Canada at the provincial and national levels since 1975. A social worker by training, in

40

1980 he had just started working as a consultant on disability issues with the Mennonite Central Committee Canada (MCC), which had its head office in Winnipeg. Through the Mennonite Central Committee, Enns gained the first contacts for funding the Steering Committee meetings of DPI (then the World Coalition). John Wieler, Overseas Director at MCC, encouraged him to contact the Canadian International Development Agency (CIDA), referring him to MCC's CIDA contact, John Mackrae.[4] Support from MCC, an organization well known to CIDA as a reliable non-governmental development and relief agency, helped the World Coalition to obtain a CIDA grant of $17,200 (Cdn.). It was granted for the World Coalition to hold the first Steering Committee meeting in Ireland in 1980.[5]

Several important decisions were made in Dublin. Ron Chandran-Dudley, a visually-impaired Singaporean, offered Singapore as the site for the founding world congress, and the Steering Committee accepted the offer. It was believed that Singapore was a good place for the congress because, while industrialized, it still belonged to the developing world. It thus provided a bridge between the developed and developing worlds.[6] The World Congress would be held in December 1981, that is, at the end of the United Nations International Year of Disabled Persons.

The Steering Committee also decided to accept the constitution written by Liam Maguire, which would be presented to the congress in Singapore.[7] The constitution was modelled on that of the International Labor Organization, since Maguire, a wheelchair-user, was deeply involved with labour concerns and with the ILO. DPI's structure would comprise five regions, with regional councils for each region, and a "world council" with five representatives from each region. Furthermore, Maguire's constitution suggested a name change for the organization to Disabled Peoples' International. The change from World Coalition for Persons with Disabilities was proposed because to the Europeans "coalition" meant a short-term agreement on cooperation between political parties to enable a government to function; it did not signal a lasting relationship. As Henry Enns reiterated, "It was felt the word coalition had a negative connotation being associated with short-term make-do arrangements characterized by instability."[8]

There was little enthusiasm and considerable skepticism on the part of some of the members before the Steering Committee meeting in Dublin. The prevailing attitude was that it would not really be possible to start an organization, yet this meeting was a turning point. There were certain occurrences that lent legitimacy to DPI. It actually received funding from CIDA, Aer Lingus then offered discounted airfares, and the Mayor of Dublin hosted the Steering Committee. Everyone left the meeting feeling determined to give this organization their best efforts to get it going.[9]

Another Steering Committee meeting was held in San Francisco on February 15–17, 1981. It was funded by the United Nations Trust Fund, which was administered by the UN Centre for Social Development and Humanitarian Affairs in Vienna, and which had been set up for the International Year of Disabled Persons (IYDP) in 1981. UN member-governments contributed to the Fund. DPI ultimately received support as a result of contacts made by Henry Enns, the DPI Chairperson, while attending UN meetings in the summer of 1980. The UN granted $21,000 (US) to bring the Steering Committee members to California, and the Department of Rehabilitation in California contributed $5,000.[10]

At the California meeting, the program for the World Congress was approved. This would focus on how to organize disabled people's organizations, issues of concern to disabled people, development and peace, and DPI's relationship to other international organizations such as the UN and the ILO. Tempers flared over language issues and this became a watershed for discontent in the Steering Committee. Tambo Camara, a French-speaking African from Mauritania, expressed his displeasure that documents sent to him were not translated from English into French. The working language of the Steering Committee was English, and all the other Steering Committee members spoke English. He had raised this in Dublin, but he felt the translation situation had not improved since that time. However, other Steering Committee members were tired of hearing his complaints. Furthermore, at this point the Steering Committee members began asking what they were going to get out of this organization, and how it would benefit their organizations. Finally, after heated debate, people began to realize that they wanted a world organization, and to organize it they had to work together.[11] It was agreed that French, English and Spanish translation would be provided when needed.[12]

There were no such conflicts at the next meeting held in Toronto on July 31 and August 1, 1981. This meeting was held with UN funds, in conjunction with a Mobility International (MI) conference. Mobility International was an international travel organization that brought disabled people together to meet each other, to socialize, and to discuss barriers to disabled people's participation. MI paid the airfare and accommodation costs of several DPI Steering Committee members who spoke at MI's conference. Some of the Steering Committee members could not be present, and thus there was no official quorum. None the less, the meeting was held because it offered the last chance to plan for the upcoming World Congress in December 1981.

A subsidy program to bring delegates from the developing world to the Singapore World Congress was discussed. The first priority was to fund the actual on-site expenses of the Congress. Secondly, DPI would attempt to fund one delegate from each country in the developing world. While it was difficult for all disabled people to obtain funding to attend a congress, it was especially so for people in the developing world because their governments and economies were also poor.

The morale at the meeting was quite upbeat. Ron Chandran-Dudley and a volunteer organizing committee in Singapore were busy making logistical arrangements. Some funds had been promised by CIDA, by the World Council of Churches and by the UN International Year of Disabled Persons Trust Fund, although these had not yet been received by DPI. Everyone thought that 200 people would be a good turnout. And at the time of the Toronto meeting, DPI had heard from thirty-six countries of their interest in attending DPI's founding congress.[13]

Promoting DPI regionally

The Steering Committee members publicized the Congress to disabled people around the world and helped groups of disabled people to organize. João Ferreira, a wheelchair-user, organized a Latin American Symposium on Rehabilitation in Costa Rica as part of his role as an International Labor Organization consultant to the Costa Rican government. He travelled extensively in Central and South America publicizing this event and DPI's upcoming Congress. Many disabled people attended the Latin American Symposium. Henry Enns, Chair of the Steering Committee, spoke at it about DPI. Some disabled participants organized an "American Association of Disabled People", a coalition of people from Argentina, Nicaragua, Venezuela and Costa Rica.[14] Jacqueline de las Carreras also organized a multi-disability organization, with a rights-oriented philosophy, in Argentina during 1981 called Corporación Argentina de Discapacitados (CADIS).[15]

In the Asian region, the Japanese organized a loose coalition of existing organizations of disabled people called the "Japan Committee for the Development of DPI".[16] They raised funds through a benefit concert, and as a result, the Japanese appeared strong in Singapore with a total of 105 delegates.[17] Senator Eita Yashiro, a wheelchair-user and former television entertainer, also raised US$60,000 for the production of a film about the Congress.[18]

In Australia, Gustav Gebels at first had difficulty in interesting people in attending the Singapore Congress. He initially approached the government-sponsored International Year of Disabled Persons group which was not a self-help group. Ultimately, however, local self-help groups of disabled people became interested in attending the Congress, and the Australian Government granted $10,000 (Australian) for twenty disabled people to attend. They joined another twenty-five interested Australians who raised their own money, and thus forty-five Australians would be able to attend the Congress.[19]

In Africa, both Steering Committee members were organizing in their regions. Tambo Camara helped complete the formation of a regional organization of disabled persons' groups in French-speaking West Africa, the West African Federation for the Advancement of the Handicapped (WAFAH), in November 1980. This coalition included organizations in Cameroon, Burkina Faso (then Upper Volta), Mali, Mauritania, Niger, Senegal, Sierra Leone and Togo.[20]

Joshua Malinga returned to Zimbabwe inspired by the happenings of the Winnipeg Congress. He had gained a clear understanding of the DPI philosophy of disabled people speaking for themselves and demanding their right to participate in society, which he shared with his organization in Zimbabwe. Malinga also spread the word about DPI's upcoming Congress in Kenya, Zambia and Botswana.[21]

Promoting DPI at the international level

Henry Enns, the Steering Committee chairperson, meanwhile publicized DPI and its philosophy at the international level throughout 1980 and 1981, and his presence at UN meetings resulted in some international visibility and funding for the fledgling DPI. He travelled to the United Nations Advisory Committee meeting for the International Year of Disabled Persons in Vienna, held on August 20–29, 1980. Enns attended as a consultant to the Canadian delegation on disability issues.

It had been due to an unexpected turn of events that it was possible for Enns to attend the UN meeting. Originally a colleague of his from

COPOH, Percy Wickman, a wheelchair-user and Co-Chair of the Canadian Organizing Committee for the International Year of Disabled Persons (COC), was to attend the Advisory Committee meeting, but at the last minute could not attend. It then looked as though other members of the Committee, who were nondisabled, were likely candidates to go in Wickman's stead. But COPOH, through Jim Derksen, Wickman and Allan Simpson, lobbied Health and Welfare Canada to send a disabled person. They wanted to send Henry Enns, who was not a member of the COC. André LeBlanc, the Director of the Bureau on Rehabilitation, also agreed that Enns, as a disabled person and Chair of the DPI Steering Committee, should go. Nondisabled members of the COC felt they should go. Ultimately, with pressure mounting on both sides, Enns received approval for his attendance from Health and Welfare Canada and was off to Vienna.

Other members of the Canadian Delegation were two members of Parliament, David Smith and Walter Dinsdale; André LeBlanc of the Bureau on Rehabilitation, and Jim Crowe from the Canadian Embassy in Vienna. There were only a few disabled people who attended the meeting. The US delegation included Frank Bowe, a deaf man who had been at the founding meeting of DPI in Winnipeg.

The Vienna meeting was important because the twenty-three-nation Advisory Committee was in the process of drafting a World Program of Action Concerning Disabled Persons (WPA) for the International Year of Disabled Persons and its follow-up. It had already held one meeting in 1979. The WPA document was to address the definition of disability, the needs of disabled people in rehabilitation, and prevention of disabilities. Enns and DPI wanted the WPA to include recognition of disabled people's right to integration and participation in society. They also wanted recognition of the importance of building disabled people's organizations.

The meeting provided a forum for Disabled Peoples' International (then called the World Coalition of Persons with Disabilities) in 1980. The Canadian delegation was supportive of disabled people's participation and organizations, and put forward a motion that Enns be granted observer status as a representative of the new DPI which was accepted at the meeting.[22] Enns was thus able to speak on behalf of DPI and represent the concerns of disabled people around the world. Overall, the support of the Canadian delegation for the principles of disabled people's participation was invaluable. It helped the fledgling DPI gain international recognition as a representative of disabled people.[23]

Enns also furthered the credibility of DPI. Being in a wheelchair added to his own credibility: by inference he knew what disabled people wanted because he himself was disabled. He managed to talk about DPI, its plans and its philosophy with many representatives of countries at coffee and lunch breaks. He encouraged them to support the participation of disabled people from their countries in the upcoming World Congress.

Indeed, by the end of the meeting, the Advisory Committee decided that a World Conference of disabled persons was needed.[24] The Trust Fund for the International Year would fund the participation of disabled people through their organizations in 1981. Thus some contacts for funding DPI activities were made, and in the end, funding for the California DPI Steering Committee meeting was secured through Enns' discussions with UN officials.[25]

In August 1981, Enns, again a member of the Canadian delegation, discussed funding for the DPI Founding World Congress with Otto Wandall-Holm, who was in charge of the IYDP Trust Fund. It looked as though funding of around $60,000 (US) would be granted.

NOTES

1   Ed Roberts, quoted in Mireya Navarro, "A Dream for a World Coalition for Disabled", *San Francisco Examiner*, February 1981, B6.

2   At this stage of organization, the leadership was mainly of a charismatic nature. According to the social movement theorist Armand Mauss, when a movement for change coalesces, or comes together, charismatic leaders take center stage. They motivate their followers. Often they also set out the philosophical underpinnings of the movement: "To what extent charisma comes from a leader's own personality traits, and to what extent it is projected by a membership or by a certain crisis situation is not clear. But he who has it is followed because the membership believes he has truth and justice on his side and that he has the right to lead them" (Armand L. Mauss, *Social Problems as Social Movements* [Philadephia: J.B. Lippincott, 1975], 6).

3   *Ibid.* According to Armand Mauss, leadership in such movements tends "to be lawyers, teachers and writers and other intellectuals, who are freer, both socially and temporally to conceive and advocate new ideas and policies" (*ibid.*, 53).

4   Interview with Henry Enns, DPI chairperson, Winnipeg, Nov. 5, 1985.

5   Romeo Maione, director general, NGO Division, Canadian International Development Agency, to Jim Derksen, executive director, COPOH, Oct. 30, 1980, DPI Development Office files, Winnipeg.

6   Henry Enns, "Report of Steering Committee", Winnipeg, November 1981, DPI Development Office files, Winnipeg.

7   DPI, "Meeting of the Steering Committee Oct. 18 and 19, 1980, Dublin, Ireland", 3, DPI Development Office files, Winnipeg.

8   Enns, "Report of the Steering Committee", 3.

9   Enns interview, Aug. 29, 1985.

10   DPI, "List of Donations and Grants to DPI (Canada) Inc., 1980–85", Winnipeg, 1985, DPI Development Office files, Winnipeg.

11   Enns interview, Aug. 29, 1985.

12   DPI, "Minutes of Steering Committee of Disabled Peoples' International in San Francisco, USA", Feb. 15–17, 1981, 2, DPI Development Office files, Winnipeg.

13   Diane Driedger and Jim Derksen, "Correspondence Report", July 1981, DPI Development Office files, Winnipeg.

14   Enns, "Report of Steering Committee", 9; DPI, "Latin American Addresses," 1981, DPI Development Office files, Winnipeg.

15   Interview with Jacqueline de las Carreras, DPI World Council member, Kingston, Jamaica, Sept. 28, 1984.

16   Diane Driedger, "From Winnipeg to Singapore", in Kathleen S. Miller and Linda M. Chatterdon (*eds*), *A Voice of Our Own: Proceedings of the 1st World Congress of Disabled People's International, Nov. 30–Dec. 4, 1981, Singapore* (East Lansing, Michigan: University Center for International Rehabilitation, Michigan State University, 1982), 5.

17   DPI, "1st World Congress 1981 Participants List", 1981, DPI Development Office files, Winnipeg.

18   DPI, "List of Donations and Grants to DPI (Canada) Inc., 1980–85", DPI Development Office files, Winnipeg.

19   "History of DPI" in Jeff Heath (*ed.*), *When Others Speak for You, You Lose: Proceedings of the First National Assembly Disabled Peoples' International (Australia) Melbourne 1983* (Adelaide: South Australian Chapter of DPI, 1984), vi.

20   Driedger, "From Winnipeg to Singapore", 4–5.

21   Interview with Joshua Malinga, DPI honorary treasurer, Kingston, Sept. 30, 1984; Driedger, "From Winnipeg to Singapore", 5.

22   Telephone interview with André LeBlanc, former director, Bureau on Rehabilitation, Health and Welfare Canada, Ottawa, June 10, 1985.

23   Henry Enns, "International Disability Issues: Canadian Involvement", Winnipeg, March 1985, 5–6, Henry Enns, DPI Chairperson, files, Winnipeg.

24   UN Advisory Committee for the International Year of Disabled Persons, "VII Recommendations, B. 'World Conference Of Disabled People', Second Session, Vienna Aug. 20–27, 1980, Agenda Item 8", 2, DPI Development Office files, Winnipeg.

25   Enns interview, Aug. 29, 1985.

5

A JOINING OF COMMON PURPOSES: THE DPI FOUNDING WORLD CONGRESS, SINGAPORE, 1981

> Our people can be found
> In every class and race
> Of every age and nation
> Our people are awakening.
>
> We will not beg
> We will not hide
> We'll come together
> To regain our pride.[1]

— Micheline Mason (United Kingdom), 1982

Disabled people came, 400 strong, from all ends of the earth to Singapore – to proclaim that they would no longer be silent. DPI's First World Congress in Singapore was a celebration of that proclamation. Many of the Congress participants had never met so many people of different cultural backgrounds or travelled so far before. Singapore was a joining of common purposes. But there were struggles involved in obtaining funds and logistics that needed to be overcome before the Congress even opened in November/December 1981.

The Canadian Secretariat searches for funds, May–December 1981

The search for funding to hold the Singapore Congress was like squeezing blood from stone, and the Congress almost did not happen. While Steering Committee members were organizing groups and publicizing DPI, the DPI staff members at the Winnipeg secretariat – Jim Derksen, Acting International Coordinator, and Diane Driedger, Administrative Assistant – worked to raise funds for the World Congress budget of almost $240,000 (Cdn.).[2] Resources to run the office came from a variety of sources. The Manitoba League of the Physically Handicapped donated some space in their Winnipeg office to DPI. The Canadian International Development Agency (CIDA) non-governmental division provided another grant of $25,000 after the California meeting for Canadian secretariat expenses and for Derksen to be employed part-time.[3] Derksen had been a staff person with disabled people's organizations locally and nationally (with the Coalition of Provincial Organizations of the Handicapped) since 1975. He was a wheelchair-user due to polio, who had an interest in eastern philosophies and wore batikked robes from Asia and Africa.

The Mennonite Central Committee Canada (MCC), in addition to allowing Henry Enns to work on DPI business as part of his job at MCC, recruited Diane Driedger as a voluntary service worker to work with DPI. Driedger was a nondisabled person, with an interest in social movements, who had worked with the Manitoba League of the Physically Handicapped in the summer of 1980.

Derksen and Driedger sent out letters to international funding bodies to raise monies for the Singapore Congress. They did this in consultation with Enns, who checked into Winnipeg every few months. Enns travelled across Canada extensively with his MCC job. None of the three had any previous experience with international organizations or funding bodies. Derksen extrapolated from his national experiences in Canada and thus steered his way through the international funding maze.

It was important to raise funds to sponsor developing world delegates to the Singapore Congress because the price of an air ticket from Africa, Latin America or even Asia could be equivalent to a delegate's annual income. Without a subsidy program, few disabled people from the developing world would be present to accept the constitution and elect a World Council representative of each region.

But DPI had difficulties in its CIDA application for funds. DPI applied to the International Non-governmental Organizations Division (INGO) of CIDA for support, and it agreed to grant $100,000 for the Congress. But DPI needed to be incorporated as a legal body in Canada to receive the grant, and even though the Canadian Secretariat had filed an application for incorporation in 1981, there were complications. Thus the CIDA money, over one-third of funds promised, was in jeopardy, as Driedger related in frustration:

Our lawyer forgot to include the name search sheet, which she had prepared, in our application for incorporation. The bureaucrats in Consumer and Corporate Affairs in Ottawa took three months to read our by-laws and then sent them back in September because of the missing name search. With the Congress and the need for funds growing ever nearer she [the lawyer] sent the name search to Ottawa. Three weeks later we were informed that we needed a limit on our board of directors and thus our application was rejected again! Infuriated, we envisioned one hundred thousand dollars slowly slipping through our hands.[4]

After this comedy of errors, an ally in Health and Welfare helped prod the acceptance of the incorporation in Ottawa, and the Letters Patent were approved and arrived in Winnipeg at the end of October. Proof of incorporation was fired off to CIDA and the Canadians waited for the money.

With less than a month till the start of the Congress, air tickets had to be purchased for developing world delegates. Some fifty disabled people were waiting at their end to hear if they would be sponsored to go to Singapore. At the beginning of November, the Canadian Secretariat had only $20,000 from the World Council of Churches and promises of funds from the UN and CIDA.

Derksen, Enns and Driedger worked out a strategy. Some risks had to be taken to ensure the representation of twenty-five developing world countries in Singapore. They arranged a line of credit with two travel agencies, one in Winnipeg and another in Ottawa. The firms paid for the tickets and sent them to disabled people in Africa, Asia, Latin America and the Caribbean. These people needed to scramble to obtain visas, permission to leave their countries, and leave of absence from jobs, all within a period of two weeks. By November 20, some fifty air tickets worth $120,000 (Cdn.) had been sent, and still the Canadian office had only $20,000. Derksen assured the travel agents that money was coming to pay for the tickets by the time the Congress started.

Thus, six days before the Congress, on November 23, the Canadians left for Singapore and took all the money they had with them. They left with travel agents waiting for payments, and with tickets sent all over the world, not knowing if they had reached their destinations. And Jim Derksen often said in those last two weeks, "We're all going to jail if that money doesn't come."[5]

Happenings in Singapore

Meanwhile, the Singapore Organizing Committee for the Congress was making last-minute hosting plans. They had received very few registration forms and thus believed that 200 people would be a good turnout. They had organized the local hosting arrangements for the international Congress in seven months. The Organizing Committee was a collection of twelve disabled and nondisabled people who were mostly professionals – doctors, teachers, business people and govern-ment workers.[6] Ron Chandran-Dudley, a family counsellor, a Fulbright Scholar, a graduate of the London School of Economics and a member of the Steering Committee, was their link to the Canadian Secretariat. The Organizing Committee booked the Hyatt Regency Hotel as the site for the Congress, and ensured that the hotel was made accessible with ramps to the front doors and into its restaurants.[7]

The Steering Committee arrived several days before the Congress to discuss last-minute details. While these discussions were going on, disabled delegates began to arrive in Singapore. The Canadians watched to see how many of the air tickets they sent had reached their destinations and it turned out that all but three people made it to the Congress. Those sponsored by the subsidy program raised the number of countries represented in Singapore from twenty-six to fifty-one.[8] Indeed, to the surprise of all the organizers, 400 disabled people arrived in Singapore for the World Congress – more than anyone had ever imagined.

These were people of various disabilities. Some were sponsored by DPI, others by governments, and still others raised money any way they could, as Kathy Miller, an American participant wrote:

Many had borrowed, sold, worked, begged – anything to raise the funds to be able to attend. Such was the man from Zimbabwe who is blind and bicycled from Salisbury [now Harare] to Bulawayo 441 km, to raise funds for his organization of the blind to send him to Singapore.[9]

Others raised enough for the airfare, and arrived with the faith that somehow DPI would pay their accommodation and meals for the week. The Canadian secretariat was approached time and time again for assistance, and it was provided.

While people were arriving, Derksen and Driedger were waiting for word from Canada that the money had arrived. They divided the money they had brought with them into meal allowances for the fifty subsidized delegates. This used the last of the money. On Thursday, December 3, one day before the Congress was to end, Derksen phoned Bill White of the Coalition of Provincial Organizations of the Handicapped (COPOH). Derksen said he was going to jail if some money was not wired to Singapore to pay the $20,000 (Cdn.) hotel bill by the next day. Derksen asked White to try to obtain a credit line at COPOH's bank and wire the money.

The previous Friday, White had heard from the United Nations that the money was coming, and he therefore went to COPOH's bank and showed them the UN telegram promising the money. But the UN funds had not yet arrived. COPOH was broke, so he arranged a line of credit for $20,000. He got Canadian External Affairs to send the money through diplomatic channels so that it would arrive faster. Indeed, it arrived the next day in Singapore, and the Canadian High Commissioner's office delivered it to Derksen's hotel room in an attaché case.[10] The money, from both CIDA and the UN, arrived in DPI's Winnipeg bank account after the Congress was over.

Meanwhile, political difficulties arose over the representation of China at the Congress. The People's Republic of China informed the Singapore Organizing Committee that it was sending five delegates to the Congress. The Congress organizers and the Steering Committee assumed that Taiwan was not attending the Congress since representatives from that country had not registered ahead of time. Thus they believed there would be no problem concerning the representation of China. Then, five Taiwanese delegates arrived unannounced. The People's Republic delegates followed a day later, and found that the Taiwanese had already begun representing the ''Republic of China,'' as their name tags indicated. The people in charge of the registration table had assumed that the Taiwanese delegates were those from the People's Republic who were expected to attend. The People's Republic delegates refused to attend the Congress unless Taiwan added ''Republic of China, Taiwan Province'' to their name tags. The People's Republic representatives stayed in their hotel rooms for the whole Congress. The Steering Committee negotiated with both sides on this matter, but the dispute remained unresolved. The Chinese, in a written statement, expressed their interest in working with all countries, while expressing their regret that they could not participate.[11] Thus international political troubles were very much a part of this meeting just as at many other international gatherings.

Yet the Congress was a joining of common purposes. Each delegate had the common experience of being disabled and wanting to be a full participant in society. The opening day of the Congress, November 30, included speeches by UN dignitaries and Singaporean government officials. Disabled people spoke on the philosophy and goals of organizations of disabled persons. Tactics for organizing national coalitions were also outlined. However, the first day ended with some delegates questioning the legitimacy of the process for accepting the draft constitution.

After the opening speeches, members of the British delegation asked to present a written statement to the Congress. But by the decision of the Steering Committee members who chaired the session, they were not allowed to do so because of insufficient time. The British felt their views were being suppressed, and circulated a written statement expressing dissatisfaction with the little time set aside for discussing the constitution. Indeed, it seemed that the Steering Committee wanted the constitution it had prepared to be rubber-stamped.

The British Council of Organizations of Disabled People (BCDOP) had mandated the British delegates to tackle several constitutional concerns. They had already obtained a copy of the draft constitution before the Congress. They had tried to speak with Liam Maguire, its author, about these issues several days before the Congress, but Maguire did not want to discuss any changes to the document he had already created.[12] Then the British delegates tried to bring up constitutional issues with Henry Enns and the Steering Committee, and felt they were being ignored.

The written statement they circulated expressed dissatisfaction with the definitions of "impairment", "disability" and "handicap" in the constitution; they were the World Health Organization's medically oriented definition.[13] They wanted a definition of handicap that explained that disabled people were handicapped by barriers in society. When these barriers, such as inaccessible buildings, were removed, disabled people would be able to participate like everyone else. They did not want disabled individuals to be blamed for their lack of participation in society; the inaccessible environment barred their full participation.

The British delegates, Vic Finkelstein, Stephen Bradshaw and Francine White, then began to lobby others who were also dissatisfied with the process. They wanted to push for time to be set aside on the Congress agenda to discuss constitutional changes. They hung posters in the foyer outside the main meeting room, calling on people to attend a meeting of "The People" that evening; the inference was that the Steering Committee members were dictators who wished to make autocratic decisions. The small room was full that night, indicating that others were at least interested in, if not supportive of the charges against the Steering Committee. Many of the delegates at this meeting also wanted time on the Congress program to discuss the proposed constitution. In the end, Henry Enns arrived at the meeting to announce that the Steering Committee had decided to suspend the regularly scheduled sessions the next day to discuss the constitution.

Emotions ran high on both sides over the constitutional issue. The

Steering Committee felt that their months of work to create a new organization might be thwarted. If the constitution was not accepted in the next four days, DPI would not be born in 1981. Other Steering Committee members felt that their authority was being questioned. They thought they had done a good job, and now the Congress delegates were unfairly criticizing their efforts. The British delegates on the other hand, believed that DPI must be based on democratic principles, and be directed by "The People", the grassroots.[14]

The next day's session became a constitutional debate as people from each of five regions of the world broke up into their regional groups to consider the constitution. In addition to the definitions of "disability" and "handicap", there was the issue of whether parents and nondisabled advocates could be a part of DPI. There was heated discussion of this issue. Some delegates from Japan did not want parents to be involved at all, they believed parents tended to over-protect their disabled children and wanted to keep them dependent – whereas, they contended, disabled people wanted to be adults, not protected children all their lives. By the end of the week, however, the constitution was accepted. The Congress participants decided that the new World Council would discuss the definition and further amendments. And parents whose children were underage and individuals chosen by mentally handicapped persons could be involved.[15] But in the end the national organization in each country would decide its own membership criteria. Of course, organizations had to be at least 51 per cent controlled by disabled people.

The Congress accepted other official documents as well. It approved the DPI "Manifesto" and a "Plan of Action" for the organization. The "Manifesto" dealt with the organization's philosophical base: "We maintain that all people are of equal value. This conviction implies that disabled people have the right to participate in every sphere of society. . . . We therefore reject all forms of segregation and we refuse to accept lifetime isolation in special institutions."[16] It also asserted the basic rights of disabled persons as citizens of the world: the right to education, rehabilitation, employment, independent living and income security. It also stated that disabled persons should have the right to influence governments and decision-making processes: ". . . organizations of the disabled must be given decisive influence in regard to all measures taken on their behalf."[17] Thus DPI had its philosophy of disabled people speaking for themselves for full participation accepted by its membership.

World problems that caused disability were discussed, as the

"Singapore Declaration" adopted by the Congress indicated: "Join us in our condemnation of policies that produce waste and destruction, policies of violence and war, policies of perpetuating disability. . . . "[18] Workshops were held on these problems, and óne workshop on disability and armanents claimed that war was the number one cause of disability. By the end of the week, the Congress passed a resolution demanding that 1 per cent of all funds spent on the arms race should go towards preventing disability. In a plenary session, the exploitative nature of multinational corporations in developing nations was cited as a primary cause of malnutrition and disability. Liam Maguire of Ireland said:

Of the world's 500 million severely disabled people, at least 100 million are severely disabled solely because of malnutrition. At least one million babies per annum die because of the misuse of powdered milk infant food, which multinational companies aggressively sell to mothers in developing countries. Four million more suffer brain damage from baby-bottle mulnutrition.[19]

Many goals were realized in Singapore. There was a feeling of liberation symbolized in the "Wheelchair Disco" as 400 disabled people danced together, a realization that all people express themselves in their own way. By the end of the week, not only were the Constitution, the "Manifesto" and the "Plan of Action" accepted, but a World Council was also elected. Representatives of the five regions of the world were elected to the governing body of DPI for four years. The World Council elected Ron Chandran-Dudley of Singapore as chairperson, and Henry Enns as deputy chairperson. Bengt Lindqvist of Sweden was elected Secretary, and Joshua Malinga from Zimbabwe became treasurer. In addition, a vice chair was elected from each of the five regions to represent regional interests. The World Council would meet once a year, and it was agreed that it would meet again in the summer of 1982.

In all, the new World Council was a continuation of the charismatic leadership elected to the Steering Committee. All but one of the original members (Gustav Gebels) were re-elected to the new Council. The criticism could be made that the Steering Committee members were hanging on to power in what was supposed to be a grassroots organization, but they had laid the philosophical and organizational framework for the organization, and inspired 400 disabled people around the world to attend the founding congress. The Congress participants decided that these leaders had demonstrated their leadership in the formative stage of DPI, and accordingly re-elected them as their representatives.

Personal goals were met for many disabled people at the Congress. Cristina Figari of Argentina organized four United Nations interpreters and one of the most senior government interpreters in Argentina to come as volunteers to the Congress in Singapore. She herself was the sixth interpreter in the team,[20] being a government interpreter in Argentina, and had obtained the qualifications to become a United Nations interpreter. Yet the UN turned down her applications for employment because she was a quadraplegic. The UN deemed workplace modifications impossible to accommodate her wheelchair. Figari proved in Singapore that she could interpret, and that the soundproof booths could be made wide enough and ramps built to enable her to gain easy access.

Other people with disabilities had never travelled outside their home-country before. In meeting people from other cultures, they discovered that concerns about disabled people's participation and equality transcended national borders. Many new friendships and romances were embarked upon. Most important, people left filled with excitement about the potential of this world voice. They carried their enthusiasm back home, and were resolved to create and build national organizations of disabled people in their countries and regions. They would also create employment and technical aids projects, and lobby government and service providers for changes.

NOTES

1   Micheline Mason, "From the Inside: A Liberation Song", in *Getting to Know COPOH* (Winnipeg: COPOH, 1987), 12.

2   "DPI World Congress Budget", 1981, DPI Development Office files, Winnipeg.

3   Henry Enns, chairperson, DPI Steering Committee, to Peter Hoffman, Non-Governmental Division, CIDA, March 12, 1981, DPI Development Office files, Winnipeg.

4   Diane Driedger, "First Voluntary Service Report from Diane Driedger to Mennonite Central Committee", Winnipeg, Nov. 14, 1981, 4, DPI Development Office files, Winnipeg.

5   Diane Driedger, "Second Voluntary Service Report to Mennonite Central Committee, A Struggle Ends, Another Continues", Winnipeg, Jan. 1982, 2, DPI Development Office files, Winnipeg.

6   "Singapore Organizing Committee Minutes", April 22, 1981–December 1981, DPI Development Office files, Winnipeg.

7   Driedger, "From Winnipeg to Singapore", 5.

8   *Ibid.*, 6.

9   Kathleen S. Miller, "A Chorus of Voices: A commentary" in Kathleen S. Miller

and Linda M. Chadderdon (*eds*), *A Voice of Our Own: Proceedings of the 1st World Congress of Diabled Peoples' International, Nov. 30–Dec. 4, 1981, Singapore, op. cit.,* 81.

10   Interview with Bill White, former COPOH national coordinator (1981–3), Winnipeg, Dec. 30, 1983.

11   Chinese Delegation, "Statement by the Chinese Delegation to the DPI World Congress", Singapore, December 1981, DPI Development Office files, Winnipeg.

12   Interview with Vic Finkelstein, British Council of Organizations of Disabled People, Nassau, Bahamas, Sept. 20, 1985.

13   British Delegation, "Statement from the U.K. Representatives", Nov. 30, 1981, 1, DPI Development Office files, Winnipeg.

14   *Ibid.,* 1–2.

15   Jeff Heath, "First World Congress of Disabled People's International – A Regional Report", 1982, 6, DPI Development Office files, Winnipeg.

16   "DPI Manifesto", 1981, DPI Development Office files, Winnipeg.

17   *Ibid.*

18   DPI "Singapore Declaration", 1981, DPI Development Office files, Winnipeg.

19   Liam Maguire, "How to Start Organizations of Disabled People" in Kathleen S. Miller and Linda M. Chadderdon (*eds*), *A Voice of Our Own,* 32.

20   Miller, "A Chorus of Voices", 82.

6

CREATING SOLIDARITY – LOCALLY AND INTERNATIONALLY

"I felt powerless before the convention but coming home I feel I've now got more knowledge, skills, contacts and enthusiasm to work for a better deal."

— participant, first Asia/Pacific regional convention of DPI, November 1984

"The leadership training seminar is very much like a process needed to make a car. We need to have four wheels, a body, and a driver before we can make a car go. . . . Now, our engines are finished. And it appears very promising. After this seminar, I hope the participating DPI leaders will have assembled fine cars which will be as good as the engines mounted, and later let each car run in his/her respective country."[1]

— Eita Yashiro (chairperson, DPI Asia/Pacific region), 1983

The disabled people who attended the Singapore Congress returned home inspired to continue building organizations in their regions. By 1985 there were disabled people's organizations, either uni-disability or multi-disability, in virtually every country of the world. The founding of DPI served to provide organizations with an international voice and an impetus to consolidate national multi-disability coalitions where none existed. After the Singapore Congress, DPI set about to increase its membership in as many countries as possible, and these organizations would enable disabled people to help themselves.

The DPI Development Program

In seeking ways to expand its membership after the Singapore Congress, DPI enacted a Development Program as its main vehicle. This Program would also contribute to the building of local and national organizations of disabled people. Its main thrust was "Self-Help Leadership Training Seminars", the rationale being that DPI would train disabled people in the developing world, where many begged for a living, to help themselves.

The idea for a development program originated at an ecumenical church service held at the time of the 1980 RI World Congress in Winnipeg. During the service delegates from the developing world related some of the difficulties they had in obtaining wheelchairs and crutches. People in the industrialized countries had many mobility aids, opportunities and services, and they left the meeting with a feeling that they should help disabled people in the developing world.[2]

In the spring of 1982, Jim Derksen, Acting International Coordinator, and Henry Enns, Deputy Chairperson, met with people in the International Non-governmental Organizations section of the Canadian International Development Agency (CIDA). Enns' portfolio as Deputy Chairperson was to investigate how to ensure that disabled people in the developing world were involved in DPI. Enns and Derksen were looking for funds for this purpose, and CIDA indicated that it could support projects that were oriented toward leadership training.[3] At the same time, the Swedes reported that their SIDA (Swedish International Development Authority) was interested in contributing about $300,000 (Cdn.) to the program.

The Canadians presented a development project proposal to the World Council in Tokyo in 1982. DPI would ask CIDA for $425,000 (Cdn.) and SIDA for $300,000 for an eighteen-month project.[4] The total program would cost $1,260,000.[5] The World Council adopted a "Self-Help Leadership Training Program" which included training exchange programs, regional training seminars, regional development officers and a small project fund.[6] This program had to be cut back because the SIDA funding did not come through as a result of a change of government in Sweden.

Nevertheless, CIDA decided to provide $90,000 (Cdn.) for a scaled-down eighteen-month Interim Self-Help Leadership Development Program, and this started in 1983. CIDA provided one-third of the funds for the project, with the Development Office channelling one-third from other agencies, and the local organizations raising one-third. The budget was over $176,500 for the total program.[7] DPI held three training seminars in its first eighteen-month program funded by CIDA. In 1983–4, CIDA granted another $250,000 for leadership training and also provided money for a small projects fund. The DPI Development Office in Winnipeg coordinated the funding. CIDA, the United Nations, Catholic Development and Peace, the Mennonite Central Committee,

SIDA and others have contributed funds. Local disabled persons' organizations raised funds for on-site expenses. Over the period 1986–9 CIDA agreed to contribute $300,000 per year. In 1989 DPI was negotiating with SIDA for a possible multi-year funding arrangement.[8] In sum, most of the program between 1982 and 1989 was focussed on leadership training.

The leadership seminars were initiated to train disabled persons to lead self-help organizations in the developing regions of the world. Self-help groups enabled disabled persons to lobby their governments for improved job opportunities, transportation, education and access to public buildings. At least three seminars have been held in each developing region – Asia, Africa, Latin America and the Caribbean – since 1982. Each of these seminars included participants from fifteen to twenty countries in the region. Experienced disabled leaders and organizers from the developing world conducted the meetings. The rationale was that after a two-week seminar the newly-trained leaders could go back to their countries and organize a disabled people's organization. Or they could use their knowledge within existing organizations to teach others new skills.

Budgetting, management, writing project proposals, leading meetings and lobbying governments and agencies for changes were all discussed. The philosophy of DPI was also affirmed. Disabled people were to speak for themselves to governments and to society.[9]

Most of all, the seminars helped disabled individuals gain a sense of self-esteem and confidence in their worth as human beings and in their own skills. At a session of the Jamaica seminar in 1987, disabled women, many of whom worked in the home, discovered that they had skills and that they should think more of themselves. As one of the disabled women pointed out, ". . . if women were homemakers they were also managers, negotiators and accountants already – they used those skills in managing a household. . . . And these skills were marketable, and disabled women could use these in the disabled people's movement."[10] Disabled people came away after meeting people with common experiences, feeling empowered – they were not alone!

An evaluation of the Leadership Training Program from 1983 to 1985 was undertaken, at the request of CIDA, to assess the effectiveness of the seminars. A team of seven people interviewed disabled seminar participants and people with UN bodies or international aid agencies who had worked with DPI. Six of the seven team members were disabled persons, who represented the different developing world regions. The evaluation revealed that the seminars had been successful in fostering skills and feelings of solidarity and empowerment for disabled people. Areas for improvement were identified. It was found too that the seminars had strengthened DPI as an organization, since they had encouraged the growth of national organizations: "Some have reported growth in membership by as much as 75%. The number of countries having some relation to DPI have grown from 41 in 1980 to over 100 in 1985."[11] For example, after some disabled people from Guyana participated in the 1983 Barbados seminar, they returned home and founded the Guyana Coalition of Citizens with Disability in October 1983.[12]

The leadership training seminars also made it financially possible for the regions to hold DPI Regional Assembly and Council meetings to make decisions. Since they were held in conjunction with the training seminars, delegates' airfares were subsidized under the training seminar program, and on-site expenses for the regional meetings held before or after the seminars were raised from other sources. But this had negative effects, as Council members were funded to attend both seminars and Council meetings. Thus funds were spent to send experienced leaders to the events, although they did serve as resource speakers in many cases. Thus, while training new leaders was the purpose of the Development Program, it appeared after three years of operation that at least half of the Program's participants were already advantaged disabled people, from which it followed that no more than half were people who had little or no leadership experience, for whom the seminars had been mainly intended.[13] In most seminars there was no representation from mentally handicapped people or those with "psychiatric disabilities" (mental illness), and males outnumbered females by a wide margin. Most of the participants were employed, more than half in mainstream jobs: these were not necessarily working with disabled people, though some did. Others were self-employed.[14] Thus there was an absence of women, of certain disability groups and of the poorest disabled people at the seminars.

There were also some difficulties in the seminar planning. The program content was too broad. Too many areas were being covered in a week-long seminar. Specific skills in accounting, fund-raising and management were not considered closely enough. The participants would have liked more intensive instruction in these areas. However, there was a problem with the different levels of skill and experience of the people who attended the seminars. This led to "unevenness in participation and at times a disjuncture between the level and choice of content and the capacity and interests of some of the participants.''[15] This happened as a result of many experienced leaders attending the seminars. In the end, the evaluation affirmed that the leadership training seminars had achieved their objectives to a large extent. Indeed, the seminar participants interviewed felt that on the whole the content of the seminars was generally what they needed. Furthermore, the effect of leadership training has been felt through the founding of multi-disability self-help organizations around the world.

The evaluation report made recommendations for the future of the development program. It was affirmed that DPI should continue it, but future seminars should include underrepresented groups: women with disabilities, those with mental and psychiatric disabilities, and the poor.[16]

Since the 1985 evaluation, DPI has addressed the needs of disabled women through separate leadership training sessions and seminars. Six seminars and sessions for women were held in 1986 and 1987, at least one in each developing region.[17] These seminars were held not only because the DPI evaluation decried their lack of participation, but because women themselves called for women's training seminars at the 1985 Bahamas World Congress. The women contended that they needed seminars focussed on the needs of disabled women because they had been ignored for so long by their communities and by disabled people's organizations. Indeed, there were few women in leadership positions in the national, regional and international levels of the self-help movement.

Regarding the inclusion of mentally handicapped people and deaf persons, only a little progress has been made. A few training seminars have included deaf people, such as that in El Salvador in 1986. But there were difficulties in communication between the deaf people and people of other disability groups.[18] And, in fact, the deaf people felt that communication barriers – the lack of others being able to use sign language, and their lack of distinct speech – made them outsiders. Some of the other participants laughed at their attempts to speak out loud. But in the end the deaf participants overrode these factors and gained some new skills.[19] Few mentally handicapped people have been involved in leadership training, but some parents of mentally handicapped children have been involved in training seminars, as in Jamaica in 1987.[20]

Poorer and less educated disabled people were becoming more the focus of attention in the training program after 1985. In the years that followed the evaluation, there was an emphasis on holding national training seminars, particularly making sure that rural people, who were often poor, were involved. There was a shift to including a majority of people who were not already leaders in the seminars. National seminars have been held in a dozen countries. And in the Latin America region a long distance Leadership Training Correspondance Course was in the process of development in 1989. This course had the potential to reach many more disabled people, as it would be cheaper to run a correspondence course than bring people to seminars in other countries. There was a possibility that this course, if successful, would be initiated in other regions.[21]

Regional Development Officers. Another regional activity revolved around regional development officers (RDOs) who were an added feature of the Development Program in 1985. They were hired to foster the creation and strengthening of disabled people's organizations. The officers hired in 1985 were Eileen Giron, a wheelchair-user, for the Central American region, based in El Salvador; Derrick Palmer, a visually-impaired person, for the Caribbean region, based in Jamaica; and Miguel Amuchastegui, a wheelchair-user, to work in the South American region, based in Argentina. The officers made contact with organizations of disabled people in their region, where they encouraged disabled people to start employment projects and to lobby their governments for changes.

The officers were successful in raising the public profile of disabled people's groups and in creating new organizations of disabled people. Derrick Palmer helped people with disabilities organize in Belize, Grenada, Trinidad and Tobago, St Kitts and the Bahamas.[22] He played the role of motivator in getting people together. Indeed, the DPI Development Program Evaluation found that, for self-help groups, "being tied to a visibly strong international body gave both individual participants and the groups they represented more credibility – both with their members as well as with governments and the public."[23] In the Caribbean, Derrick Palmer's visits helped disabled people's organizations to gain credibility with their governments. Often, when Palmer, a social worker by training, came to visit different Caribbean countries, meetings were arranged with the country's Prime Minister or President, as in Guyana and Trinidad. Representatives of the local disabled people's groups went along to these meetings too. These officials learned that the disabled people's movement had a credible international and regional base.[24] DPI, after all, had consultative status with the UN's Economic and Social Council (ECOSOC) and ties with other international bodies. Thus, governments perceived local and national disabled people's groups as having clout.

By 1989 only one development officer remained who was funded by the Development Office, Derrick Palmer in Jamaica. And he was taking on additional responsibility as North American/Caribbean regional director, which dealt with DPI's organizational and political matters in the region. Funding for the Latin American posts had run out. In the future the regions will continue to attempt to locate funding on a local basis to enable the concept of Regional Development Officers to continue. In 1989 there were regional offices in Africa, one in Zimbabwe for the anglophone countries and one in Mauritania for the francophone countries. Both these offices have received funding from CIDA, above the regular DPI Development Program budget. In Europe, a regional office has operated in the HCK office in Sweden since 1987. At the time of going to press, the Asia/Pacific region was in the process of setting up a regional office in Thailand.

International Symposium on Development, Jamaica, 1984. DPI also sponsored an International Symposium on Development in Kingston, Jamaica, in October 1984. Its purpose was to begin discussions between representatives of disabled persons' organizations and development agencies. Of the ninety people who attended the meeting, over half were from disabled people's groups. Unfortunately, few of the invited development agencies were able to attend. Many appeared reluctant to spend funds attending a conference, and one is bound to wonder whether possibly the agencies simply viewed disabled people's issues as unimportant. Yet another factor contributed to the agencies' poor attendance, namely that DPI sent out invitations for the event only four months before it was to take place, and development agencies had already made plans for that length of time.

However, at the Symposium DPI shared its view that it was important to build organizations so that disabled people could help themselves in the development process. Overall, the participants agreed that disabled people and development agencies should work together in planning projects for disabled persons. Both parties had skills and experience that could be shared, and disabled people, DPI participants believed, were often those best placed to know their needs in development.

The European Region. The DPI Development Program only attempted to set up organizations in the developing regions. The European Region was not included in this program at all for funding or leadership training.

In addition, the European members were not able to raise funds for organizational development in Europe. Only nine countries were members of DPI by 1989.[25] There had been no leadership training seminars once a year to which organizations could be invited, and to help finance DPI internal meetings in Europe. They did not have money readily available to enable them to meet; even in Europe, disabled people were the poorest of the poor.

Europe had a wide array of organizations of disabled people, many of which had existed longer than organizations in other parts of the world. But most of them did not join DPI. However, lack of development money was only one reason why the European Region was so under-represented in DPI. Another reason was the existence of a regional disability coalition in Europe, the Fédération International des Mutilés, des Invalides du Travail et des Invalides Civils (FIMITIC). This grouped seventeen organizations of disabled people across Europe. According to Simonetta Bencini, of the Italian organization, Associazione Nazionale Mutilati ed Invalidi Civili,

We never contacted DPI directly; it may do a good job, but as we joined FIMITIC in 1953 and are cooperating in its different Commissions we do not feel the need to join another organization with similar goals.[26]

Indeed, FIMITIC had the same goal as DPI: disabled people them-selves must speak out for their own integration and equality.[27] It also had consultative status with ECOSOC, UNESCO, the ILO and the WHO. The European organizations that belonged to FIMITIC could compare similar experiences, and use them to improve legislation in their own countries. Indeed, with an organization already existing in Europe, why should European organizations join DPI?

People within DPI, on the other hand, claimed that FIMITIC was not a strong organization. It was not represented at UN meetings, such as those for the drafting of the World Program of Action Concerning Disabled Persons. They claimed it was more an organization on paper, not active and certainly not activist.[28] Furthermore, it was primarily composed of mobility-impaired people; with other disability groups remaining unrepresented. Jan Johnsson, of the DPI secretariat, further stated that as an organization, FIMITIC was dying; it did not have the enthusiasm that DPI had about working for the equality of disabled people.

FIMITIC, on the other hand, claimed to represent all disabled people, and to have people of all disability groups involved in the organization. It believed that it provided a mechanism by which European organizations could share information and expertise on issues that they had in common. It argued further that disabled people in Europe had their own unique perspective, and thus European organizations benefitted from sharing with each other. They would not necessarily benefit from sharing with disabled people in other regions. But FIMITIC did not bar organizations in other regions from membership,[29] and it had corresponding members in other regions.

FIMITIC's head secretariat was funded through membership fees, and received no funding from other sources. The congresses that FIMITIC held every four years were funded by the national hosting organizations, all of which were in Europe. There were no funds to subsidize delegates who could not afford to attend, and thus developing world corresponding members would find it difficult to attend congresses. Thus it appears that it would not be easy for disabled people in regions outside Europe to participate in FIMITIC.

As for attendance at UN meetings, FIMITIC was not present, as already mentioned, at the World Program of Action Concerning Disabled Persons discussions, nor at the ILO meetings on the Vocational Rehabilitation Convention. This happened to be impossible due to a reorganization FIMITIC was undergoing at the time. In the final analysis it believed it had a big enough struggle to ensure that disabled people in Europe gained their dignity and the right to a decent standard of living.

Overall, the prior existence of FIMITIC, coupled with the lack of money for meetings, slowed down the European Region's participation in DPI. The death of Liam Maguire of Ireland, the vice chairperson for Europe, in 1983 also created a vacuum, and there was no one responsible for pulling together the European Region till 1985. The DPI secretariat in Sweden made some efforts, but it was already understaffed, and thus organizing its European dimension was not its first priority. As already mentioned, a regional office for Europe was initiated in the office of DPI Sweden (which includes the HCK in its membership).

Socio-economic projects

The DPI Development Program promoted leadership training that would help disabled people to start and maintain not only organizations but self-help projects. Most organizations in DPI did not have any funding from government, especially those in the developing world. So they set about raising seed money from non-governmental organizations to start self-sustaining projects. DPI's Development Program had an indirect impact on the development of some projects by making it possible for disabled people to meet each other and share project ideas. For example, at the Barbados 1985 Training Seminar, people from Guyana, after talking with others who were running employment projects, were inspired to start their own. In 1986, the Guyana Coalition of Citizens with Disability started a hatchery run by disabled people, which was expected to provide employment for twenty to thirty disabled people, as well as providing food and funds for others who would receive fifty to one hundred chickens per year. They could sell the chickens and this would provide a good profit because meat was expensive in Guyana.[30]

But DPI did not always fulfill the expectations or the needs of disabled people either. Some African leaders attended the 1984 DPI Symposium on Development in Jamaica, where development agencies and disabled persons met. They brought along project proposals, hoping to find an interested funding agency. However, most people were disappointed, because many development agencies did not attend, and because most of the time was spent discussing philosophical issues. In general, too, some Africans were disappointed that their disabled people had not benefitted financially from being affiliated with DPI.[31] However, DPI did not view its role as one of finding funds for its members. Its focus was on providing contacts so that disabled people's organizations could find their own funding for projects.

Indeed, on the whole DPI's influence in starting socio-economic projects was indirect. Ideas were refined at DPI seminars and meetings, but the groups themselves contacted funders in their own countries and development agencies interested in working with them. The following examples were initiatives undertaken in different parts of the world.

In 1984, the National Council of Disabled Persons of Zimbabwe (NCDPZ) started an outreach program to locate disabled people in the rural areas and help them to organize, and to start projects. First of all, the NCDPZ's outreach staff travelled in the rural areas and identified and talked to disabled people. As a result, there were many instances of disabled people in a given area forming small groups, which would become branches of the NCDPZ. There were no conditions for membership in the NCDPZ, and thus it encouraged nondisabled persons to be involved too. It was open to those who supported the NCDPZ's philosophy of integration into society, and disabled people speaking out on their own concerns. The outreach workers also carried out public education in the communities. They talked to village leaders, church people, doctors, government officials and the peasants to convince them of the need to integrate disabled people.[32]

The local disabled people's groups continued to locate disabled people in their areas and to encourage them to join. Many rural groups worked on small projects which both helped them to obtain skills and brought in some revenue. The most popular projects were small-scale animal raising and vegetable growing, and there was spinning, weaving and sewing. The NCDPZ headquarters staff raised funds to start these projects, and Horticultural Therapy and Rural Training in England, an organization promoting rural agriculture and crafts, helped with its expertise in starting small agricultural projects.[33] These projects meant that a disabled person could be productive in the community and be integrated into its economic activities.

In Nicaragua, the Organization of Disabled Revolutionaries (ORD), started by people disabled in the Sandinista revolution, ran a wheelchair workshop where disabled people built wheelchairs and crutches on contract for the national government. It also started a sewing cooperative, where both disabled and nondisabled people worked. This provided employment for disabled people in an integrated environment.[34]

Several groups began projects in the Caribbean, in addition to the hatchery in Guyana. Since 1981, the St Lucia Council of the Disabled has started a popsicle-making business and a fruit drink business. The marketing strategy was to take advantage of opportunities, as Tony Avril of the Council explained: "In St Lucia, the tourist industry is perhaps the second big money-making thing there. But are disabled people benefitting from it? The answer is no."[35] Thus, they found a market selling popsicles and fruit drinks to tourists.

The Combined Disabilities Association (CDA) in Jamaica started a wood products factory making toys and ornaments in 1983. About 60 per cent of its workers were disabled, and the other 40 per cent nondisabled. The profits from the factory would be used to sustain the CDA's operations and it also benefited the twenty disabled workers economically and in skills training. This project has been assisted by volunteer staff, both from the Mennonite Central Committee and from CUSO. It has also received some financial assistance from the Christian Blind Mission based in West Germany. The CDA also operated a revolving loan scheme, funded by the Netherlands government, to provide loans for disabled people to start small businesses. Since

1983, disabled people using the fund have started restaurants and shoemaking, tour boating, furniture refinishing and poultry farming businesses.[36]

Disabled people in developed nations also started projects to benefit themselves. In Canada and the United Kingdom, independent living centers were founded between 1982 and 1989.[37] These centers were based on the same premise as those started in the United States in the 1970s. They were run by disabled people to help other disabled people to live as independently as possible in the community. Attendant care, peer counselling and information and referral about existing services were some of the features of the centers.

In addition, both North American and European organizations of disabled people contributed to development projects in the developing world. In some cases, these projects were undertaken independently of DPI. The Norwegian Association of the Disabled provided funds for a meeting of organizations of physically disabled people in Africa.[38] Likewise, HCK (Handicappförbundens centralkommitté) in Sweden has provided funds for the running of the office of the National Council of Disabled Persons in Zimbabwe.[39]

In Canada, three provincial chapters of the Coalition of Provincial Organizations of the Handicapped (COPOH) have "twinned" with organizations in the developing world. In such a relationship, organizations share expertise and resources for the benefit of disabled people in their countries. People United for Self-Help in Ontario (PUSH) in Kingston, Ontario, twinned with Jamaica's Combined Disabilities Association in 1984 with the help of staff and financial resources from CUSO.[40] The Voice of the Handicapped of Saskatchewan twinned with Nicaragua's Organization of Disabled Revolutionaries in 1984. Saskatchewan sent wheelchair parts to Nicaragua. The Manitoba League of the Physically Handicapped, again with the aid of CUSO, twinned with the Guyana Coalition of Citizens with Disability in 1987. There have also been exchange visits between groups.

In all, disabled people in the developed world felt a need to help others with fewer resources, but they also helped for philosophical reasons. Georgina Heselton of the Voice of the Handicapped of Saskatchewan explained:

It is important for the disabled to work together on an international level to build a broad movement. As Canadians we can get to know the hardships of disabled people in developing countries, but also the striking similarities between us, in the obstacles we face.[41]

Indeed, the Swedes concurred with the concern for all disabled people, and added that they learned from other movements:

It is our belief that disabled people will benefit from the exchange of information through the world network of DPI, as well as contributing to international solidarity by assisting sister organizations to build up in developing countries.[42]

Finland contributed directly to DPI Development Program efforts. The Kynnys ry (The Threshold), a group of disabled people in Finland, raised money from their government to support DPI's development activities.[43]

Disabled people mainly started socio-economic projects on their own without the direct input of DPI. They raised funds from development aid agencies and began their own self-sustaining projects. It would appear that DPI's leadership training efforts had an impact as disabled people used their own skills to benefit their organizations and themselves.

Overcoming societal barriers

DPI was also, on the whole, not involved directly in the lobbying efforts of national and local organizations. However, its training seminars did provide places where disabled people could share their lobby efforts in their countries with others. They thus imparted information on how to approach issues, and created solidarity among disabled individuals who realized that they faced similar barriers in their own countries. Indeed, disabled people lobbied their governments, businesses and the public for the elimination of the attitudinal and environmental barriers to their participation. The following are some instances of their activities.

In Canada, the Coalition of Provincial Organizations of the Handicapped was successful in having the rights of disabled persons included in the federal Human Rights Act in 1983. In 1981, COPOH also lobbied the Government to have the rights of disabled people included in the new Canadian Constitution. Their rights were entrenched in the constitution's Charter of Rights and Freedoms.[44]

In Jamaica, the Combined Disabilities Association (CDA) undertook several successful awareness campaigns. It has done public education work about the abilities and rights of disabled people, mainly through a newsletter and a weekly radio show.[45] It negotiated with the government about housing options for disabled people in the community. This led to the government committing 5 per cent of some new public housing apartments to be accessible to disabled persons. And interest payments were waived by the government in 1981 on the purchase of some units.[46]

In Argentina, the Corporation of Disabled People (CADIS) has been conducting awareness sessions with the university architectural school in Buenos Aires.[47] Their premise was that to create a physically accessible society, architects needed to be educated about physical barriers (such as stairs) and how to overcome them in architectural design.

In December, 1981, the Government of Pakistan enacted the Disabled Persons Employment Ordinance. The Pakistan Association of the Blind had lobbied for this for ten years, and, as Dr Fatima Shah explained:

This ordinance, apart from other things, ensures 1% quota of jobs for the disabled in all public and private institutions in Pakistan, along with suitable training facilities for them.[48]

In Nicaragua, the Organization of Disabled Revolutionaries (ORD) conducted a campaign to increase public awareness about the need for wheelchair accessibility. Transportation, in particular, was a problem for disabled people since buses had steps and were not accessible. Taxis were the main transportation for disabled Nicaraguans. Many taxi-drivers refused to carry disabled passengers because they did not want to be bothered with helping a person transfer from the wheelchair into the car and then loading the wheelchair aboard. ORD has been working with taxi cooperatives to end this discrimination.[49]

The foregoing organizations, and others around the world, have been raising awareness about their accessibility needs with governments and the public. These have been almost entirely local and national efforts. DPI's contribution has been in creating international solidarity, and partly as a result of this, developed countries in Europe and North America have helped in the projects of their disabled sisters and brothers in the developing world. DPI has also made a contribution through its Development Program and its international political involvements. But DPI needed to continue to build an international organizational infrastructure to enable itself to confront issues at UN forums and to be a philosophical resource to its membership. It had set out to create an international organizational infrastructure after the Singapore Congress.

NOTES

1   Jeff Heath (*ed.*), *The Adelaide Experience: Report of the First Asia/Pacific Regional Convention of Disabled People's International, Nov. 1984* (Adelaide: DPI Australia, 1985), 20; Yukiko Oka (*ed.*), *The Engines Are Ready, Let's Go! Report of DPI Asia/Pacific Leadership Training Seminar* (Tokyo: DPI Asia/Pacific Regional Council, 1983), v.

2   Derksen interview, June 15, 1986.

3   Interview with Henry Enns, DPI chairperson, Winnipeg, Nov. 5, 1985.

4   Derksen interview, June 15, 1986.

5   Aldred Neufeldt *et al.*, *An Emerging Voice, Report to Disabled Peoples' International on its Self-Help Development Program* (Winnipeg: DPI [Canada], 1985), 2.

6   Derksen interview, June 15, 1986.

7   DPI "Report 1983", 2–3, DPI Development Office files, Winnipeg.

8   Interview with Paula Keirstead, DPI chief development officer, Winnipeg, March 2, 1988.

9   Yukiko Oka (*ed.*), *The Engines are Ready, Let's Go!*; Jeff Heath (*ed.*), *Developing Leaders: Report of Disabled Peoples' International Leadership Training Course, Adelaide, 1984* (Adelaide: DPI [Australia], 1985).

10 Irene Feika, quoted in Diane Driedger, "A Mutual Sharing: The Disabled Peoples' International (DPI) Leadership Training Seminar in Jamaica, July 1987", unpublished, Sept. 1987, 4, Henry Enns files, Winnipeg.

11 Neufeldt *et al.*, *An Emerging Voice*, 16.

12 Joseph Skeete, "Guyana Coalition of Citizens With Disability Report", *ca.* 1986, Henry Enns files, Winnipeg.

13 From surveying existing participants' lists of five of the seminars, there is an indication that just over half of the participants had not been leaders in organizations before. And the Zimbabwe seminar in 1985 was composed mainly of existing leaders.

14 Neufeldt *et al.*, *An Emerging Voice*, 9.

15 *Ibid.*, 36.

16 *Ibid.*, 35–7.

17 Interview with Henry Enns, Winnipeg, Dec. 2, 1987.

18 Interview with Paula Keirstead, Winnipeg, Dec. 17, 1987.

19 *Ibid.*

20 Enns interview, Dec. 2, 1987.

21 Hugo Garcia Garcilazo, "Latin America Regional Chairperson's Report", to DPI World Council Meeting in Stockholm, August 1987, 6–7, Henry Enns files, Winnipeg.

22 Henry Enns and Derrick Palmer, "North American/Caribbean Regional Report," *ca.* 1985, Henry Enns files, Winnipeg; Carlton Stevenson (chairperson), "Grenada Council of the Disabled (GNCD)", Oct. 31, 1986.*

23 Neufeldt *et al.*, *An Emerging Voice*, 16.

24 Interview with Derrick Palmer, DPI regional development officer for North America and the Caribbean, Winnipeg, April 22, 1986.

25 Cyprus, Denmark, Finland, the Netherlands, Norway, Poland, Portugal, Sweden and the United Kingdom.

26 Simonetta Bencini, Associazione Nazionale Mutilati ed Invalidi Civili, to Diane Driedger, Oct. 9, 1986, 1.*

27 Fédération International des Mutilés, des Invalides du Travail et des Invalides Civils (FIMITIC), "FIMITIC" (pamphlet), Paris, *ca.* 1986.*

28 Telephone interview with Jan Johnsson, head of DPI secretariat, Stockholm, Nov. 18, 1986.

29 Marija Stiglic, secretary general, FIMITIC, to Diane Driedger, March 4, 1987.*

30 Interview with Henry Enns, Winnipeg, Oct. 31, 1986; Joe Skeete, "Lecture to an Open Meeting of the Manitoba League of the Physically Handicapped" at Society for Manitobans with Disabilities, Nov. 10, 1987; "DPI North American and Caribbean Region Third Biennial Regional Leadership Training Program, 1987, July 20–25, Kingston, Jamaica", 3, Henry Enns files, Winnipeg.

31 Zogo Menye Alphonse, president, Union National des Handicapés du Caméroun, to Jan Johnsson, head, DPI secretariat, June 24, 1986, Henry Enns files, Winnipeg.

32 Joshua T. Malinga, "The Silent Majority" in Diane Driedger (*ed.*), *The Winds of Change: Partners in Development, Proceedings of the DPI International Symposium on Development, 1–5 October 1984* (Winnipeg: DPI [Canada, 1 1985]), 50.

33 National Council of Disabled Persons of Zimbabwe, "Outreach Program Project Description", *ca.* 1984, 3.*

34 Coalition of Provincial Organizations of the Handicapped (COPOH), "Interview with Georgina Heselton, Saskatchewan Voice of the Handicapped", *Info COPOH* (June 1986), 2.

35 Tony Avril, "Community-Based Projects in St Lucia" in Driedger (*ed.*), *The Winds of Change* (Winnipeg: DPI [Canada], 1 1985), 60.

36 Huntley Forrester, "Report on DEEDS Industries" in Driedger (*ed.*), *The Winds of Change, op. cit.*, (Winnipeg: DPI, 1985 4); Combined Disabilities Association, "Eleven Get CDA Loans", *Mainstream: Newsletter of the Combined Disabilities Association, Ltd* (Sept. 1983), 4.

37 April D'Aubin (*ed.*), *Defining the Parameters of Independent Living* (Winnipeg: COPOH, 1985); British Council of Organizations of Disabled People, "Centres for Integrated/Independent Living, Prepared for BCODP AGM and Conference", Sept. 1985.*

38 A. Eidhammer, "Disabled People Must Organize!", *The African Rehabilitation Journal* 2 (July 1985), 2–3.

39 Joshua T. Malinga, "National Council of Disabled Persons of Zimbabwe, Chairman's Report to the Annual General Meeting held at Park Lane Hotel, in Harare on July 16, 1983", 1983, 1.*

40 Wayne Westfall, "Jamaica – And Its Disabled", *CUSO Forum* 2 (Nov. 1984), 4.

41 COPOH, "Heselton Interview", 2.

42 Peter Lamming, international secretary, DPI Sweden, to Diane Driedger, Oct. 17, 1986, 2.

43 "Acknowledgements", Driedger (*ed.*), *The Winds of Change*.

44 Diane Driedger, "Speaking for Ourselves: A History of COPOH on its 10th Anniversary" in *COPOH 1985–86 Annual Report* (Winnipeg: COPOH, 1986), 21.

45 Westfall, "Jamaica", 4.

46   Combined Disabilities Association, "CDA Info Sheet", *ca.* 1984, 5, DPI Development Office files, Winnipeg.

47   Interview with Jacqueline de las Carreras, DPI World Council member, Kingston, Jamaica, Sept. 28, 1984.

48   Dr Fatima Shah, "Up-to-Date Report of Work in South Asian Region", *ca.* 1984, DPI Development Office files, Winnipeg.

49   Medical Aid to Nicaragua, "What is *ORD?*", 1985, 2.*

7

GROWING PAINS: INTERNAL OPERATIONS

"The best of all rulers is but a shadowy presence to his subjects . . .
Hesitant, he does not utter words lightly.
When his task is accomplished and his work done.
The people all say, 'It happened to us naturally.' "[1]

— Lao Tzu (551–479 BC)

The process of building DPI's infrastructure was fraught with conflicts, tensions and inexperienced judgements along the way in the first four years of its existence, 1981–5. However, after emerging from those years, it appeared, in 1986–9, to be on the road to greater stability.

Internal operations, 1981–85

Throughout this period, DPI's internal operations and politics were characterized by five trends. First, the World Council was in large part a continuation of the "old boys' " Steering Committee network that excluded certain groups. The Steering Committee members were all elected to the new World Council, except for one member, Gustav Gebels from Australia. Half the Council, and all but one of the executive positions, were filled by the old Steering Committee members. Indeed, this group was very much an élite clique that held much of the power in DPI. The original Steering Committee had only one woman going into the Singapore Congress and no representative of the deaf or mentally handicapped communities. These groups had been underrepresented in Winnipeg at the RI World Congress in 1980, where the Steering Committee was elected.

Secondly, the power dynamics in the new World Council were affected by conflicts between Executive members who had known each other since the Steering Committee stage. A battle between the visually-impaired and mobility-impaired also carried over from the Steering Committee in more acute form after the Singapore Congress, as one Executive member was blind and the other mobility-impaired. While DPI was a coalition pledged to include persons of all disabilities, disability groups tended to coalesce into blocs of influence. This tension was compounded by a rivalry between the staff of DPI's two main offices in Sweden and Canada.

Finally, amidst these points of tension, the leadership of DPI struggled to initiate a new international infrastructure. Most of those involved were relatively inexperienced in the task of international organization-building. All the foregoing factors affected the operations of DPI as an organization from 1981 to 1985. Often they proved disruptive, and many of the Council meetings of the organization were preoccupied with political manoeuvrings and power struggles within the organization. This dissipated energies and resources that DPI could have expended outside the organizational infrastructure to challenge societal barriers. The following sections explore these five trends.

World Council. The World Council elected in Singapore included, as already mentioned, all but one of the Steering Committee members. Thus ten of the Steering Committee members were returned to the twenty-two-member Council. Certain regions, such as North America and Europe, did not have a full complement of five members on the Council. This was due to the European Region having only three representatives of self-help groups in Singapore when the Council was elected. Also, only four countries from the North American/Caribbean region were represented in Singapore. The inadequate representation of these regions was partly due to disabled people from the developed regions being ineligible for DPI sponsorship because they were not from so-called poorer countries. Many disabled people from Europe and North America could not afford to travel to Singapore and were unable to raise money on their own to attend.

The World Council included five women, and the African region did not have a woman on the Council. The ages of these members were thirty-five to sixty-six years old, with the greater proportion being thirty-five to forty-five. The disabilities represented on the Council were: mobility-impaired (17), blind (6) and deaf (1).

While mobility-impaired men were strongest numerically on the Council from 1981 to 1985, the blind persons' group was stronger than its numbers indicated. This was due to several factors. Two key players in the Steering Committee, Ron Chandran-Dudley and Bengt Lindqvist, became Chairperson and Secretary respectively, of the new Council. Because they had previous international experience with Rehabilitation International and the International Federation of the Blind, they had credibility and influence within the disabled people's movement and in the Council. The remaining three Executive members – Henry Enns, deputy chairperson; Joshua Malinga, treasurer; and Ann-Marit Saeboenes, publications and information secretary – were mobility-impaired.

In the subsequent functioning of the Council at its four World Council meetings in Japan, Sweden, Jamaica and Bahamas, two camps were mobilized within the Council. Blind people tended to support one another within the World Council, and likewise mobility-impaired people banded together. These conflicts did not bring the activities of the organization to a halt, but they resulted in poor communication within the Council and slowed down the implementation of activities. And the conflicts led to a siege mentality on both sides.

An atmosphere of distrust emanated from the Executive in the period 1981–5. Conflicts existed between two of the Executive members over four issues: the differences in the perspectives of the developing and the developed worlds, leadership style, the World Congresses, and the administrative offices in Canada and Sweden.

First, the conflict between the two Executive members was exacerbated to some extent because one of them was from a developing country and the other from a developed one. There was some belief on the part of the former that persons from the developed world, including the other Executive member, had had access to greater monetary resources and, because of this, had control of the "pursestrings" for DPI. On the other hand, the developed world Executive member and World Council members believed that they were handling the money they received as equitably as possible. Furthermore, many of the African and Asian Council members did not believe that people from developed countries were controlling the pursestrings. These differing points of view served, to some extent, as a backdrop to the Executive members' conflicts on other DPI issues.

Secondly, leadership styles clashed from the first meeting of the Council in Singapore. Overall, members of the World Council felt that leadership style was reflective of DPI as an organization. On the one hand, some members of the World Council preferred leadership by one person through the Chairperson. They felt that strong leadership from the Chairperson showed that the organization was behind that person and knew where it was going. The Chairperson, in essence, embodied the organization at different international functions and in the media. However, other members of the Council believed that DPI should have collective leadership, in other words that those persons on the Executive should take direction from the grassroots of the organization, and implement their needs and desires. The function of the Chairperson in a collective leadership model was to coordinate the efforts of the grassroots, the regional councils and the members of the World Council.

Thus, at the World Council meetings between 1982 and 1985 there were conflicts between these two perspectives. If the members' perspectives on leadership had been similar, the Council meetings would have run more smoothly. The leadership style debate heightened the level of mistrust involved in reporting on the Singapore Congress, and in the planning for the World Congress in the Bahamas in 1985. To some extent, the mismanagement of these two issues damaged DPI's credibility with the United Nations, international funders and the disabled people's constituency.

World Congresses. Singapore and Bahamas. Two World Congresses held respectively in 1981 and 1985 were different in character. The Singapore Congress served to add momentum to the DPI movement, while the Bahamas Congress was poorly organized and thus drained energy from the membership.

According to the DPI Constitution, a Congress must be held every four years. The World Congress was not a policy-making body, but rather a forum for discussion of pertinent issues for disabled people and their organizations. However, because the First World Congress of DPI in Singapore was held to accept the Constitution, "Manifesto" and "Plan of Action" for DPI, it was a policy meeting. However, it was agreed in the World Council, and stated in the Constitution, that subsequent Congresses would not make policy. Rather, they would be forums of discussion to give the World Council ideas about which issues were important to disabled people. These Congresses were open to any disabled people who wanted to attend, as well as to representatives of international organizations, such as UN and other international aid agencies, which were interested in DPI.

There was a problem of representation at the Singapore Congress in 1981. Delegates were chosen in a haphazard way to attend the Congress. People sponsored by the Canadian Secretariat were mainly from disabled people's organizations, but in some cases they were merely individuals wishing to attend. Some who attended and were elected to World Council were later accused of misusing their organizations' funds, or they were not representative of the self-help group in their country.

Overall, however, the Singapore Congress was a resounding success if measured by the enthusiasm and the momentum it gave to organizations of disabled people around the world. But difficulties over the reporting of the Congress arose soon after in 1982. In was decided in Singapore at the first World Council meeting in 1981 that Michigan State University's University Centre for International Rehabilitation would edit and publish the proceedings of the Singapore Congress. Indeed, the University Centre would bear most of the cost of putting out the report in book form. Thus the editors of the proceedings attempted to obtain copies of all the papers presented, but their letters were not heeded and they decided to include all the papers they had and to write summary chapters about the events, people and atmosphere of the Congress. It was not a typical conference proceedings, as it was to be a tool for inspiring disabled people to organize.[2] When the report appeared in the fall of 1982, it looked very professional, and was well-edited, but several World Council members were disturbed by the portrayal of several events in the report. First, they felt that the presentation of the political conflicts over the representation of China showed a naiveté about world events. Secondly, some World Council members believed that the inclusion of a commentary on the personal conflicts involved in the constitutional battle which ensued about definitions was inappropriate. The Council decided that the report was not the official report of the Congress and that DPI would publish an official proceedings for the Congress on its own.[3] This was undertaken, and in 1985 the English report of edited papers was published. The printing of French and Spanish versions was still awaited in 1989.

The disagreements over the appropriateness of the Congress report caused problems for funders and hurt the international credibility of DPI. One funding agency, which had supported the Singapore Congress, has since not granted any more funds to the organization. It believed that it should see a final report and a proceedings of this Congress before it would grant any additional money.

The controversy surrounding the report can be chalked up to the inexperience of the fledgling DPI in producing such reports. Indeed, the final draft was not circulated to all the World Council members before it was published.

There were also problems with the film about the Singapore Congress that was made with funds from the Japanese Shipbuilders Foundation. When some of the Council members saw the final version of the film, they were not pleased with the editing job, and decided that it could be done better in Sweden. The Swedes took a year to produce a new film, and again the impact of the Singapore Congress was lost. Also, the film produced in Sweden turned out to be a promotional film for DPI, discussing its philosophy, goals and objectives for the future, not a film about the Singapore Congress. Some of the World Council members were unhappy that the momentum of the Singapore Congress had been squandered.

In the planning for the Bahamas World Congress in 1985, difficulties were also encountered. Planning for the event began only four months before it was to be held, due to the World Council's lateness in accepting the Bahamian group's offer to host the World Congress. As late as the World Council meeting in Jamaica in September 1984, the decision had still not been made. This was due to the two Executive members disagreeing among themselves about where the meeting should be held. One member supported Bahamas, while the other wanted it held in Vienna, close to UN offices. Others in the organization felt that the Disabled Persons Organization in Bahamas was too new, small and inexperienced to host such a major event. But there were questions too as to whether the disabled people's organization in Austria would be any more experienced than the Bahamians.

By the end of the World Council meeting in 1984, however, the Bahamian Disabled Persons Organization was asked to be the next hosting organization of the World Congress. The actual planning for the meeting only began in the spring of 1985 when the Bahamian group formed an organizing committee. Fund-raising for an international subsidy program also began in 1985. There was also little time for local fund-raising in the Bahamas. As a result, DPI emerged from the Congress with a deficit. Furthermore, the Congress accommodation, transportation and program were disorganized. This frustrated many participants, some of whom asserted that the lack of coordination interfered with discussing issues of concern to disabled people. Some representatives of governments, the UN and development agencies made the same assertion. This once again hurt DPI's credibility.

In addition to local difficulties and DPI's disorganization, the United Nations again promised funds and delivered them during and after the World Congress, as in the case of the Singapore Congress. This time it caused suffering for disabled Africans, many of whom did not receive their tickets from DPI in time to attend. Others borrowed money to buy tickets and were reimbursed after the Congress. All of this caused anxiety for those delegates sponsored by DPI.

From these experiences the Council realized that planning for the next

World Congress in 1989 must start as soon as the 1985 Congress was finished. They realized that staging an international event required enormous energy on the part of the DPI offices and the local organization. Sufficient time was needed to raise funds and to arrange local accessible travel and accommodation for disabled people. Organizing an international conference was a feat for any organization. But logistics for disabled people included extra planning to guarantee accessibility of facilities and support services, such as attendant care.

Administrative problems. The inexperience and disorganization reflected at the Bahamas World Congress also characterized the DPI administrative offices in the period 1981–5. These growing pains were a function of building a new international infrastructure. But the conflicts between the two Executive members discussed above also affected the functioning of the organization. It contributed to poor communications between the two main DPI offices in Canada and Sweden. Also evident in the relationship between the offices was the deepening tension between the staff of the two offices. There was one office in Canada, responsible for development projects, and there was another in Sweden, which was the head secretariat. The Swedish secretariat handled membership matters, internal communication and external communication with the UN and international bodies.

Misunderstandings often arose between the two offices concerning their roles in the organization. The heads of the offices – the Head of the Secretariat and the Chief Development Officer – had equal ranking in the organization, but often the question of who had authority over which areas was unclear. They also wondered whether information was being shared between the offices openly. The misunderstandings had their roots in the Singapore World Council meeting in 1981, where it had been decided that Canada would continue to retain the secretariat of the organization for six months because it currently had the necessary resources to continue the secretariat's function. They also agreed that the new location of the secretariat would be decided at the next World Council meeting.[4] This understanding about who would take on the secretariat function was not clear to everyone in the organization. Because the secretary of DPI was Bengt Lindqvist from Sweden, there was an assumption on the part of some Council members that the secretariat of the organization should be in the country where the Secretary himself resided. From December 1981 to the next Council meeting in Tokyo in June 1982, there was some conflict between the

Canadian and Swedish offices because of this confusion. In the spring of 1982, the Swedish government provided funding for a secretariat in Stockholm, and there was pressure from some World Council members to start moving the secretariat functions of the organization to Sweden before June 1982. At the same time, funding for a development program from the Canadian International Development Agency seemed quite likely by the time of the Tokyo Council meeting in June. Thus the Canadian office could become the development office.

In the meantime, both offices suspected the motives of the other. This included a belief that the other office was hoarding information about what was happening in DPI, and was compounded by the fact that the Steering Committee Secretariat had been in Winnipeg, and thus the Canadian office felt a sense of ownership. Furthermore, while the Swedish disabled people's delegation had promised in 1980 in Winnipeg to fund a Steering Committee secretariat in Sweden, it never materialized. At that point, the Steering Committee decided to create the Canadian secretariat. Overall, the Canadian office was disappointed in the efforts of the Swedes. In the end, the Swedes took over the secretariat function for DPI. And the Canadians took over the development office function.

The feelings of mistrust were in many ways precipitated by the rivalry between the two Executive members, who aligned themselves with one or the other of the offices. The mistrust meant that the offices did not keep each other informed of their activities. Copies of letters were not shared regularly. There was also a reluctance to talk on the phone to those with whom they felt uncomfortable. This siege mentality continued up till the Bahamas World Congress in 1985, when a new World Council and Executive were elected.

The decision to have two main offices came about largely as a result of funding bases in Sweden and Canada. As mentioned earlier, CIDA granted a sizeable sum of money to the development office. This funding was contingent on the office remaining in Canada. Likewise the Swedish government granted a total of $417,462 (US) for the DPI secretariat from 1982 to 1985.[5] The ongoing commitment of the Swedish government for this office was $110,000 per year. In addition, it paid 90 per cent of two support staff salaries, totalling some $23,000 a year. The deputy chairperson has been responsible for the Development Office, and the secretariat in Sweden has been responsible to the honorary secretary of DPI.

Internal operations, 1986–89

The fires of disorganization and conflict that had raged following the Singapore Congress were largely extinguished in 1986. And DPI rose, strengthened, from the ashes. At the 1985 Bahamas World Congress a new World Council and Executive were elected. The problem of the "old boys" returning to power was to some extent solved. The World Council members, five from each region, were elected by DPI's five Regional Assemblies before the Bahamas Congress, and these Councils had chosen some people who were new to DPI. The DPI Constitution outlined that each of the five regions would elect their own Council members at a Regional Assembly where delegates from all the DPI member-countries in that region would be represented. This helped to ensure grassroots participation. Indeed, the membership of countries in each DPI regional structure had risen dramatically since 1981. And the Regional Councils elected by these countries were planning their Development Program activities and forwarding these plans on to the Development Office in Canada.

Furthermore, only two of the five-member DPI Executive had been on the previous Executive – Henry Enns, now chairperson, and Joshua Malinga, the deputy chairperson, both elected in 1985. Much of the tension in the Executive was then dissipated because one of the two members who had been in conflict was no longer on the Executive. And generally, the 1986–9 Executive was concerned about working cooperatively and as a collective leadership for DPI. It decided at its second Executive meeting in February 1986 that the officers would act as a management team, and not in "honorary roles". Instead, they would do a great deal of the work and the supervision of the staff required for their area of Executive responsibility. Thus, for example, the deputy chairperson would supervise the work with the Development Office, the secretary would supervise the activities of the secretariat, and the treasurer would work on the budgets with the secretariat. The chairperson would coordinate everyone's responsibilities.[6]

After the 1985 World Congress, DPI had considered hiring a secretary general, preferably a person with a disability, to coordinate the staff supervision and political activities of DPI. But the Executive decided that it wished to take on that overall responsibility, because it wanted to make the political representations and it was also difficult to find a suitable candidate for Secretary General.[7]

Nevertheless, DPI's administrative problems were not resolved overnight. It took about a year for the offices to begin to trust each other. The staff realized that they needed to work hard at restoring trust between their offices, so that communications and the overall administration of DPI would improve. Furthermore, there was a recognition that the two-office structure, with each holding equal status, contributed to the conflicts. The two heads of the offices realized that there would be grey areas of jurisdiction, but they agreed that communicating on a regular basis would avoid most misunderstandings. Indeed, communication between the offices, and within the organization, has improved since 1985. DPI's acquisition of telex, computer and telefax equipment also facilitated speedy communication. And ultimately, DPI decided in the spring of 1988 to reorganize its structure to resolve the difficulties of having two offices with equal status. The Head of the Secretariat became responsible for both offices and the position was renamed ''Administrative Director''. The chief development officer became the ''Development Program director'' and the Development Office in Canada would report to the administrative director in Sweden. The administrative director would then report directly to the chairperson and the World Council.[8]

DPI has also addressed the administrative problems in organizing World Congresses every four years. The DPI World Council asked DPI members to apply to hold the Congress, and in July 1986 it chose Bogota, Colombia, as the 1989 venue. The Council decided that local organizations needed years, not months, to plan such a world meeting, and accordingly the Colombian organization, the Asociación Colombiana de Personas Impedidas, worked over a long period at local fundraising and the accessibility of the Congress site.

Underrepresented groups

In DPI's eight-year existence, its month-to-month functioning has largely been directed by the administrative offices and the Executive. The World Council, however, met once a year to make policy decisions for the organization. In this group deaf people, women, youth and mentally handicapped and mentally ill people were underrepresented, or not represented at all. In particular, deaf people and women expected that an organization concerned with the rights of all disabled people, regardless of disability or gender, would be concerned about their representation and their role in decision-making. DPI, however, fell short of their expectations, and thus both a deaf person's representative and women asserted their right to be heard and to have an equal role in the organization.

Deaf people's participation. There were few people with hearing impairments at the First World Congress in Singapore, and none was elected to the first World Council from any of the regions. Therefore, after the Singapore Congress the Asia/Pacific region decided to co-opt a deaf woman, Manfa Suwanarat, who was one of those most closely involved in the development of sign language in Thailand, to the World Council. Throughout the years that she sat on the Council, there were difficulties concerned with the needs of a person with a hearing disability because other Council members had mobility or visual impairments, and clearly the Council had to be educated in this matter. They basically understood that people who were profoundly deaf, as was Suwanarat, required sign language interpreters in order to understand the meetings. In Tokyo in 1982 Suwanarat brought one interpreter who was paid for by DPI. The interpreter was her key to understanding and communicating with everyone during the meetings. She and her interpreter found that one person to interpret the ten days of meetings was insufficient, because he became very tired after interpreting for sixteen hours in one day.

Thus, at the Swedish World Council meeting in 1983, a resolution was presented at the meeting calling for two sign language interpreters for any deaf World Council member. It was agreed that funds would be raised to bring along these two people with the deaf person, because sign language can differ totally in different countries. There is no international sign language, hence it was not acceptable to hire interpreters in the country where the meeting was being held. Also, the national sign language of a deaf person was very important to the culture of that person. Suwanarat knew only Thai sign language.

The question of deaf people's participation in DPI still remained a burning one after the 1985 Bahamas World Congress. There were few deaf individuals in attendance at the Congress. In fact, those who were represented mostly lived locally in the Bahamas.

After the Bahamas Congress there were no deaf people on the World Council and their participation in national organizations has been minimal. DPI has made some effort to include deaf people in its training seminars, but this has not been a widespread effort. However, DPI has been looking at ways to work with the World Federation of the Deaf.[9] But the task of recruiting members of the deaf community into national organizations of disabled persons, and into DPI, still remained a crucial task for the future.

Women's concerns. Women's involvement in DPI from its beginnings has also been minimal. Only three of the original Steering Committee members were women. Five women were represented on the twenty-one-member World Council of DPI, the governing body, from 1980 to 1985, but only two were elected to the new World Council for the period 1985–9; however, another five were appointed after it was recognized by the participants in the 1985 World Congress that they were poorly represented. Of 250 delegates to the Congress seventy-five were women, and the developing regions had very few women delegates. For instance, out of twenty African delegates there was only one woman.

Disabled women's concerns first arose at the World Council meeting in Stockholm in 1983. Women with disabilities were not well-represented on the World Council or on the regional bodies of the organization at that time. Therefore, in Sweden a resolution was put forward calling for more women

to be involved in the organizations of disabled people on local, national, regional and international levels and that they should be included in all national, regional and international delegations in order to provide them with an opportunity of acquiring experience and knowledge to improve their situation.[10]

The women's question was not resolved at that point.

A year later at the World Council meeting, another resolution concerning women's participation came forward. It resulted from women's meetings held outside the regularly scheduled sessions of the meeting. At the meetings the women expressed concern that there were few women involved in the executives and governing bodies of national organizations of disabled people or of DPI. The resolution called for measures to include women on executive bodies and national councils in DPI member-countries. It stated: ''The ultimate goal of this process is to bring the percentile representation of women on national councils to 50%, in accordance with their representation in the population.''[11] The resolution called, further, for leadership training seminars to be held, which would focus exclusively on the women's concerns.

At DPI's Second World Congress in the Bahamas, disabled women again met to discuss their concerns over equal representation. They presented a resolution to the organization requesting 50 per cent representation in its decision-making structures.

The delegations with the largest percentage of women at the Congress were from Canada and Australia. Both these delegations in fact had a majority of women. The Canadian and Australian women arranged meetings outside the scheduled Congress sessions, to which they invited all women with disabilities. Sixty women met and shared information about the participation and representation of disabled women in their countries. They agreed that disabled women had difficulty speaking out in disabled peoples' organizations that were largely controlled by men; many women lacked the confidence to speak out at meetings where men were present, and thus men tended to dominate. This was so, for example, on the Congress plenary floor, but at the women's meetings many women felt comfortable about speaking out. The women also discussed the lack of marriage opportunities for disabled women in the developing world, where marriage and family were often the only source of status for women. It was concluded that in both developing and developed world countries, society did not view disabled women as sexual beings because their bodies were not perfect.[12]

After the first meeting, the women set up a committee to draft a resolution for equal participation by women in DPI, and this was presented on the plenary floor by the end of the week-long Congress. During its presentation, Dr Fatima Shah, a sixty-nine-year-old physician and former senator from Pakistan, and a member of the drafting committee, warned that disabled women might separate from DPI, just as DPI had separated from Rehabilitation International five years earlier. Dr Shah had been present at the formation of the International Federation of the Blind in 1964, when it separated from the World Council for the Welfare of the Blind. Indeed, since 1981 there had been little movement on DPI's part towards including more women in decision-making or leadership training.

The resolution on equal participation was referred to the DPI World Council, which agreed that five women, one from each of the five regions of the world, be co-opted or appointed to it. The resolution also called for the increased representation of women to up to 50 per cent at least, at the regional and national levels of the organization. To assist this process, the resolution proposed that leadership training seminars be held for women in the developing regions through DPI's Development Program. During 1982–5 nine seminars had been held, but the majority of participants had been men. Disabled women wanted some seminars to be held which would be aimed at their own concerns and needs.[13] In addition to these measures, the World Council created a Standing Committee on Women's Affairs to which it elected Dr Fatima Shah as chairperson. This Committee would monitor implementation of the resolution, and disseminate information on what disabled women in all regions were doing to address their concerns.

There were varied responses to the women's agitation for more participation in the decision-making bodies of DPI. A few women did not involve themselves in the women's meetings, apparently not wishing feminism to be aired at a Congress on disability, or the Congress to be seen as speaking out on women's issues only. They wanted DPI to be concerned with issues affecting disabled people as a whole.

Men from developed Western countries tended to acknowledge the legitimacy of the women's concerns, and some spoke out on the floor in favor of the women's demands. The new Chairperson, Henry Enns, was asked during his campaign speech for chairperson what he would do for women and what his record had been on women's issues. He said that he had worked for women at home in Canada, and that this was indicated by the majority representation of women on the Canadian delegation to the Congress. However, another man from the North American region described the demands of the women at the Congress as a "tempest in a teapot".[14]

There was also a mixed reaction from men of the developing world. At a plenary session, a man from Asia asked the "women to keep reminding us of your rights. I have a mindset that I have developed not to think of them." Several men from Latin America affirmed that women had an integral role to play in society, but a statement that "behind every great man is a great woman" was met with boos. When the resolution for more women's participation was introduced on the floor, some Africans abstained from voting. Otherwise, the resolution in favor of exploring measures for more participation was unanimous.[15]

The women's issue was a difficult one for African men, who often still regarded women as wives whom they owned and who did their bidding. Women had few rights in many African societies, with children automatically becoming the property of the father. However, this was slowly changing; in Zimbabwe, for example, a new family law was giving women more rights over their children than they had had previously. In fact, Africans were beginning to realize that women must be involved more in the African disabled people's organizations in order that the organizations would be representative of all disabled persons.

Since 1985, at least one leadership training seminar geared towards women has been held in each developing region. Furthermore, in 1989 ten of the thirty World Council members were women – one-third in contrast to one-fifth in 1985. This was due to each region co-opting a woman and the Regional Councils electing some new women representatives to the Council. And many national disabled people's organizations have taken the women's issue seriously – those in Zimbabwe, Mauritania, Jamaica, South Korea, Thailand, New Zealand, Australia and Canada have formed women's caucuses.[16] Women have discovered through these caucuses and through leadership training that they have something to contribute to society, and are discovering increasingly what they need and want for themselves. An Asian man at the South Korean Women's seminar in 1986 asked, "What do you women want? To be equal to able-bodied women? To disabled men? Or to able-bodied men?" To which Dr Fatima Shah asked, "What do you want?" He said, "I want to be equal to anybody." She replied, 'We want the same.' "[17]

Organizational issues

While there were conflicts and representation difficulties, there were also housekeeping duties for DPI. Membership and constitutional issues have been debated and decided upon in the whole period since DPI was founded in 1981.

Membership issues. Fifty-one countries were represented at the Singapore Congress, and fifty-eight at the Bahamas Congress in 1985. By 1989, DPI had sixty-nine members, which were national organizations of people of various disabilities, and had contacts in fifty other countries. Its membership included only a few countries from Europe and only one country, Poland, from Eastern Europe. Complications over the representation of China in Singapore probably set back Chinese membership, but DPI affirmed at its Tokyo World Council Meeting in 1982 that it wished the People's Republic of China and not Taiwan to be a member of DPI; after all, the UN recognized the People's Republic (PRC) and it had millions of disabled people. However the disabled people's organizations in the PRC have been cautious about joining DPI, although they have shown interest in the organization.

There was also controversy regarding South Africa's membership. This first arose at the World Council meeting in Jamaica in 1984. The World Council was split on the issue. On the one hand, Vic Finkelstein of Britain, a wheelchair-user and an anti-apartheid activist, himself a South African by background, was against South Africa's membership, which he believed DPI should not accept while apartheid remained in existence. On the other hand, some Africans, notably Joshua Malinga of Zimbabwe, believed that South Africa should be allowed some type of affiliation with DPI. He explained that the South African federation of disabled people included both black and white people in its membership. Furthermore, he argued, DPI should include South Africa because disabled people there were experiencing the same difficulties as disabled people in any other part of the world, and apartheid created especially harsh conditions for black disabled people, who were poor and unemployed. And indeed, many people had become disabled as a result of the apartheid system, for example in the course of clashes during anti-apartheid demonstrations. The issue was hotly debated, and in the end DPI decided not to welcome the participation of South Africa while the current system of apartheid existed.[18]

The issue came up again at the 1987 World Council meeting in Sweden, and again Malinga was a strong supporter of DPI granting some kind of organizational status to Disabled People South Africa (DPSA). He reiterated that DPSA was working against apartheid, having walked out of a government-sponsored symposium for South Africa's own International Year of Disabled Persons in 1986; it had said it would only participate in the meeting if it was recognized that apartheid was the biggest cause of disability and of the unequal sharing of resources in South Africa.[19] Finally, Malinga argued: "[DPSA] is really part of the liberation movement. It is controlled by the blacks and the inspiration of the movement is from the blacks in Soweto."[20] Indeed, the members of the DPSA had pointed out to Henry Enns on his trip to Africa in 1987 that the African National Congress was recognized by other countries as a liberation movement, so why could not the DPSA be viewed as a liberation group for disabled people, which was against apartheid?[21]

In the end, the Council recognized that the DPSA did not support apartheid and thus granted it observer status according to UN precedents for anti-apartheid organizations from South Africa. This meant that the organization would not have voting rights in DPI, and would only have speaking rights at the World Council at the Council's invitation.[22]

While there was no provision for observer status in the DPI Constitution, this would be worked into constitutional revisions that were to be prepared for the 1989 DPI World Congress in Colombia.

However, the South African membership issue arose once again at the 1988 World Council meeting in Thailand. Huntley Forrester, a World Council member from the North American and Caribbean Region, had abstained from voting on the issue in 1987, maintaining then that the regions had not had the chance to discuss South Africa's membership in their Regional Councils. He believed the issue should be taken back to the regions before any decision was made. Thus in 1988 he presented it to the North American and Caribbean Regional Council, which decided that it did not wish DPI to grant observer status to South Africa. First of all, the observer status was not allowed for in the DPI constitution, so how could DPSA be granted this status? Secondly, the Region maintained that no organization with "South Africa" in its name should be part of DPI, as South Africa did not allow most of its citizens to vote for its government. Its view was that it would accept a group from South Africa which did not overtly represent the country by having its name in the titles of its organization. After all, the African National Congress, as a resistance movement, did not have "South Africa" in its title. Ultimately, the 1988 World Council meeting decided that the granting of observer status to DPSA would be held in abeyance until the constitution's amendments could be finalized in 1989. In the meantime, DPI was to continue informal contacts with disabled persons and their organization in South Africa.[23]

Constitutional changes. DPI has revised its constitution when this has proved necessary. Right after the Singapore Congress the World Council had the responsibility of enacting the constitutional amendments that were agreed on there. When the Council met in Tokyo in 1982, amendments to the constitution were discussed. The major changes involved definitions. The original DPI Constitution accepted the World Health Organization's definitions of "impairment", "disability" and "handicap", but many of the World Council members and people at the Singapore Congress did not agree with these definitions which, they thought, reflected a traditional medical model view of disability, handicap and disabled people. They asserted that the physical and social environment, and not their own disabilities, handicapped their participation in society. It was decided in Tokyo that a new definition would be substituted for WHO's definition in the Constitution.

The definition adopted in Tokyo stressed that handicap was a relationship between an individual and his/her environment; thus the onus has not placed on disabled people for their lack of participation in society. The definition as accepted was as follows:

a. Disability is the functional limitation within the individual caused by physical, mental or sensory impairment, and *b*. handicap is the loss or limitation of opportunities to take part in the normal life of the community on an equal level with others due to physical and social barriers.[24]

DPI wanted these new definitions incorporated in international documents relating to disability, especially at the United Nations. It believed that when a minority group had its own definition of itself accepted, it had won a basic step towards self-determination for the lives of its members. Disabled people had defined themselves, and they wanted the world to accept their definition. They wanted society to cease to point to the disabled individual for his/her lack of participation, and instead to break down the barriers that it had erected. These barriers were on the one hand paternalistic attitudes, and on the other the physical inaccessibility of the goods and services enjoyed by the rest of the population.

Generally, then, DPI experienced internal conflicts and some mismanagement in its operations during its first years. The mishandling of resources such as leadership, membership and its World Congresses hurt its credibility with some of its members, notably women and deaf people, but possibly this was only to be in the short term. Its credibility with other international organizations was also hurt to some extent, but was enhanced by its strong representations at international policy-making forums, as will be seen in the next chapter.

NOTES

1   Lao Tzu, *Tao Te Ching* (Harmondsworth, England: Penguin Books, 1963), 73.
2   Kathleen S. Miller, University Centre for International Rehabilitation, Michigan State University, to Liam Maguire, Dec. 10, 1982, DPI Development Office files, Winnipeg.
3   DPI, "Minutes of the DPI World Council Meeting, Stockholm, Aug. 15–25, 1983", 10–11, DPI Development Office files, Winnipeg.
4   DPI, "Minutes, World Council Meeting Dec. 4, 1981, Singapore", 1, DPI Development Office files, Winnipeg.

5   DPI, ''Simulated Statement of Revenue and Expenditure for the Combined Canadian and Swedish Operations for the Year Ended 31 March 1985'' in DPI, ''Minutes World Council Meeting the Bahamas, Sept. 15–17, 1985'', DPI Development Office files, Winnipeg.

6   DPI, ''Minutes DPI Executive Meeting, Sacramento, Calif., Feb. 18–20, 1986'', 9, Henry Enns files, Winnipeg.

7   Interview with Henry Enns, Winnipeg, Dec. 2, 1987.

8   Enns interview; interview with Paula Keirstead, DPI chief development officer, Winnipeg, Dec. 17, 1987; April 12, 1988.

9   Enns interview.

10 DPI, ''Minutes Swedish World Council Meeting, 1983'', 14.

11 Diane Driedger (ed.), *The Winds of Change* (Winnipeg: DPI [Canada], 1985), 72.

12 Diane Driedger, ''Women with Disabilities Meeting,'' in ''Notes on the Sessions of the DPI Bahamas World Congress'', Winnipeg, Sept. 18, 1985.*

13 ''Appendix 2, Resolution Adopted by the World Council Concerning Women's Issues, Sept. 23, 1985,'' in ''Minutes of the World Council Meeting, Nassau, Bahamas, Sept. 23, 1985'', DPI Development Office files, Winnipeg.

14 Driedger, ''Notes'', Sept. 18, 1985, 4–5, and Sept. 20, 1985, 1–10.

15 *Ibid.*, Sept. 20, 1985, 1–10, and Sept. 21, 1985, 1.

16 Enns interview.

17 Keirstead interview.

18 DPI, ''Minutes of the World Council Meeting in Kingston, Jamaica, Sept. 24–27, 1984'', 8, DPI Development Office files, Winnipeg.

19 Joshua Malinga, ''South Africa Issue: Presentation to the DPI World Council'', Aug. 1987, 203.

20 *Ibid.*, 4.

21 Henry Enns, ''South Africa Situation'', Chairperson's Report to DPI World Council, Aug. 1987.

22 DPI, ''Minutes DPI World Council Meeting, Stockholm, Aug. 10–14, 1987'', 10–11.

23 DPI World Council, 1988, ''Resolution on South Africa'', Bangkok, Thailand, August 1988.

24 DPI, ''Constitution'', 1985, 1, DPI Development Office files, Winnipeg.

8

CITIZENS WITH RIGHTS:
INTERNATIONAL ACTIVITIES

"We, the disabled people, demand the right to speak for ourselves at this and all other international gatherings."[1]

— Henry Enns (Canada) at Rehabilitation International World Congress, 1980

Whether DPI was marching on to the main floor of the UN General Assembly's Third Committee, lobbying for its position at UN and International Labor Organization (ILO) sessions, or exposing the Nazi-engineered holocaust against disabled persons, it was successful in representing disabled people's views and in garnering some policy changes.

DPI was concerned with four key issues in its representations to international forums. First, disability definitions were a DPI concern in the drafting of international documents and in meetings on disability. The debate over definitions was carried out at the meetings on the UN World Program of Action Concerning Disabled Persons and at the ILO's meetings on a Vocational Rehabilitation Convention and Recommendation. Again, disabled people rejected the medical definition of themselves and reiterated instead that the physical and social environment excluded them from participation.

Secondly, DPI was concerned that the UN and governments worldwide should recognize disabled people's self-help groups as consultants on disability issues; it maintained that disabled people were the best judges of what were their own needs and concerns. DPI gained recognition through achieving consultative status with the UN Economic and Social Council (ECOSOC), the UN Educational, Scientific and Cultural Organisation (UNESCO) and the ILO. Thirdly, DPI, with consultative status, had some ability to influence the outcome of disability-related issues at the UN. It was with this status that DPI participated at the UN Human Rights Sub-Commission.

Fourthly, international peace had to be an important issue, because war and fighting were a prime cause of disability. DPI thus called for funds spent on the arms race to be re-directed towards socially useful purposes.

94

DPI involvement at the United Nations

DPI had two goals at the UN from 1981 onwards. The first was to gain consultative status with ECOSOC and other UN bodies such as UNESCO, the WHO and the ILO. Consultative status enabled non-governmental organizations, such as DPI, to make presentations at UN meetings. It also meant that the UN organizations would consult DPI on international issues related to disability.

Secondly, DPI attended UN meetings to gain credibility for itself as a powerful voice of disabled people that should be consulted on disability matters, and in this role it achieved some success by influencing UN policies regarding disabled persons. Most important, DPI could define the needs and desires of disabled people internationally by being their rightful voice.

Consultative status with ECOSOC, UNESCO and WHO. DPI obtained Consultative Status with the United Nations through ECOSOC on May 12, 1983.[2] Under ECOSOC there were UN agencies, such as the United Nations Children's Fund (UNICEF) and the United Nations High Commissioner for Refugees (UNHCR).

DPI prepared an application for consultative status stating how it could advise and cooperate with the programs of the UN and its related agencies.[3] Ron Chandran-Dudley, Chairperson, and Henry Enns, Deputy Chairperson, appeared before the Committee on Non-Governmental Organizations at the UN in New York on February 10, 1983. DPI had applied for "Category I", the highest degree of status, and at the Committee meeting all the members recommended this category except for France and the Soviet Union. Their feeling was that DPI was a very young organization.[4] The Soviet Union was also concerned that much of its funding came from governments and that it was concerned with only one area of ECOSOC activities, namely disabled people. DPI replied that it was concerned with a whole range of human activities:[5] these would be the issues of war and peace, occupational safety and malnutrition. Other countries agreed that DPI was concerned about many issues, but the nineteen-member committee needed unanimity to approve Category I, and thus Category II was granted instead. This was a disappointment, since it meant that DPI would not be able to bring up new agenda items at UN meetings. However, Category II still guaranteed DPI representation at UN headquarters in New York and to UN offices in Geneva and Vienna. DPI would also receive UN documents and newsletters, and was allowed to comment on international issues at the UN and meetings of its bodies.

In addition, UNESCO granted DPI Consultative Status, Category "C", on August 6, 1985. This meant that DPI and UNESCO would share information.[6] But because Category C was the lowest degree of relationship, DPI could be an observer at meetings and express its views to UNESCO, but could not vote at UNESCO meetings. (Category A would give an organization the right to present proposals, vote and speak; in Category B an organization could vote and speak.) It usually took organizations several years to be elevated to a higher level, and at the time of writing DPI had not attained a higher category.[7]

In May 1985, DPI applied for consultative status with the World Health Organization. DPI and WHO had already had informal discussions on various disability issues, and WHO representatives had taken part in DPI seminars and Congresses, but the process for gaining consultative status was that an organization and WHO needed to have worked together in informal consultations for several years. DPI was still in line for consultative status at the time of writing.[8]

DPI was consulted on several of WHO's projects. It had input into the WHO manual, *Training the Disabled in the Community*, the first draft of which was issued in 1979 and distributed for field testing to evaluate its effectiveness. In 1980, the manual was amended aftèr consultation wtih disabled people, and with rehabilitation and community health experts. It continued to be tested till 1982 in the Philippines, India, Sri Lanka, Mexico and St Lucia.[9] The community-based rehabilitation (CBR) program aimed to provide disabled people in developing countries with education, jobs and involvement in community life:

CBR promotes community responsibility and reliance on local resources. *Family and community members* take care of the essential training for their own disabled, using local technology. . . . The community with its leaders takes on the responsibility for making necessary changes in the physical environment in order to give the disabled freedom of access. It also takes on the responsibility of positively influencing societal attitudes to further the acceptance of the disabled as equals.[10]

The program introduced local people to a training package that helped disabled people to live more independently in the community, and was largely successful, since 73 per cent of those who benefitted from training from 1979 to 1982 in nine countries were disabled people.[11] The CBR approach was taken due to the fact that only 2 per cent of the disabled population received institution-based rehabilitation in the big cities. Most disabled people in rural areas received no physical rehabilitation, aids or vocational training. Thus the goal was to move away from putting up large buildings and toward keeping disabled people in the community with all other adults, disabled and non-disabled.

DPI also agreed with the WHO study that services should be provided for disabled people to remain living in their communities. Large residential institutions, it believed, were a relic of the past, and independent living was the wave of the future. DPI has recommended that parents should be involved in training and disabled individuals themselves employed as teachers in CBR programs, since they know best what are the difficulties of other disabled people through their own experience with disability. In fact, DPI encouraged the CBR program to involve national and local disabled persons' organizations in its implementation.[12]

World Program of Action Concerning Disabled Persons. "More than a policy document, the World Program of Action (WPA) is a declaration of emancipation. . ."[13] was the description given by Henry Enns, who was involved in its drafting. The WPA was indeed important for disabled people's rights. It was the UN's official policy statement on disability, calling on the governments of the world to implement its recommendations. The WPA promoted full participation in society for the world's disabled people. DPI pushed for a new definition of "handicap", for disabled people to be viewed as citizens with rights, and for organizations of disabled people to be recognized as the voice of disabled people. It was largely successful in having its views incorporated in the WPA, and its international credibility was raised during the drafting of the WPA.

The first draft of the WPA, prepared in 1980, emphasized medical rehabilitation and the medical model that assumed disabled people needed to be cared for all their lives. When it was discussed at the 1980 RI World Congress in Winnipeg, many disabled people took part and criticized the document. They wanted to change its medical-model orientation and philosophy – disabled people wanted to be involved in and consulted about their lives.

Henry Enns attended the meetings in 1981 and 1982 concerning the WPA as an adviser on disability to the Canadian delegation. He was also allowed, with the backing of the Canadian delegation, to represent DPI, which at the time had no formal status at the UN. He brought concerns about the draft WPA to the meeting, and his influence, along with that of Frank Bowe, a deaf American from the disabled people's organization in the US, and the support of the Canadian and Swedish delegates, caused the committee to discard the 1979 draft. It then prepared an outline for a new document based more on the model of full participation of disabled persons, also emphasizing that disabled people's organizations should be consulted about policies that concern their own lives. Thus, even though the WPA was to be completed for 1981, the International Year of Disabled Persons, the twenty-three-country committee decided to redraft it in that year. At the 1981 meeting a drafting committee was set up to redraft the WPA, and the Canadians Henry Enns, André LeBlanc and Jim Crowe (the last-named from the Canadian embassy in Vienna) were appointed. After it was drafted, the Swedish and Canadian delegates (including Bengt Lindqvist of DPI among the Swedes) lobbied with other delegations for its acceptance. The draft upheld DPI's stand: "The concepts of consumer involvement, consultation, and support for organizations of disabled people were clearly in evidence in this first draft."[14] Between the meetings in 1981 and when the Committee met again on July 5–14, 1982, its members shared the. WPA draft with organizations in their (twenty-three) countries and with their governments. In July 1982, at the UN Advisory Committee meeting, the WPA was adopted and it passed the UN General Assembly later in the year.

The WPA accepted in 1982 was not based on the medical model, which held that the professional was the expert and disabled people were merely recipients of care. The WPA affirmed that "disabled people are first and foremost citizens with rights, and secondly, clients of social services (paragraph 25). As citizens they have every right to benefit from the social and economic developments in their countries."[15] Thus the philosophy of the WPA was that disabled persons as citizens with rights

have the right to participate fully in society and utilize community service[s] the same as every other citizen. Thus the World Program of Action is based on the principles of human rights, full participation, self-determination, integration into society and equalization of opportunity, while the traditional model was based on segregation, institutionalization, and professional control (paragraph 18).[16]

Because the WPA was based on citizens' rights, the responsibility was placed on governments for ensuring those rights. Governments were to exercise the appropriate leadership, and provide resources to implement the WPA in their countries.

The WPA also emphasized the need for involvement of disabled people in decisions that affected their lives, and thus consultation had to take place with organizations of disabled people. The WPA supported the formation of such organizations.[17]

DPI did not have its views incorporated in one area, that of the definitions of "impairment", "disability" and "handicap". As mentioned previously, in its revised Constitution it rejected the WHO definitions. DPI believed that "handicap" was a relationship between the society, its social and physical barriers, and the disabled individual. But the WHO definitions were used in the WPA as the result of a split in the UN Advisory Committee on which definition to accept. A compromise was reached when the WPA called on WHO to reexamine its definitions in consultation with disabled people.[18] And indeed DPI did send representatives to WHO discussions about definitions in 1985. Most of the nondisabled participants appeared satisfied with the existing definitions, but it was agreed that discussions about definitions would continue in the future. Also, the meeting recognized that disabled people needed to take part in the discussions. Vic Finkelstein, a DPI representative to the 1985 meeting, felt that disabled people's input was important on this occasion:

Able-bodied people have often enough said, quite rightly, that there should be no taxes without representation. I believe that we must say to the WHO and anyone else concerned that there should be no disability taxonomy without our representation![19]

Thus DPI greatly influenced the drafting and acceptance of the World Program of Action. Both the process of acceptance and the document itself were significant both for DPI and for disabled people internationally. DPI's credibility as an international voice for disabled people had been proved because it was granted observer status at three of the Committee's meetings. It gained support from governments for its stand, initially Canada and Sweden and then the other Committee members. In the process, DPI also gained some funding for its First World Congress, as mentioned in Chapter IV. Members of the Canadian Delegation also spoke well of DPI to the Canadian Departments of External Affairs and Health and Welfare. This boost helped DPI in Canada and its ability to obtain funding for its Development Program from the Canadian International Development Agency.[20]

Without DPI's input the WPA would not have had so great an

emphasis on financial support for organizations of disabled people or on the environment being the cause of disabled people's inability to participate fully in society. International bodies and documents may not have much impact worldwide, but they are among the few mechanisms for world cooperation available. When the World Program was accepted in 1982, it was then up to DPI's national members to influence their governments to implement the WPA in their countries.

UN Decade of Disabled Persons, 1983–92. In the process of lobbying for the UN and governments to act on the principles of the World Program of Action Concerning Disabled Persons, a dozen disabled people flooded into the UN General Assembly's Third Committee in 1987. Even by then, few governments had yet attempted to implement the WPA or had even recognized that there was a Decade of Disabled Persons to do it in.

The UN Advisory Committee for the International Year of Disabled Persons (1981) had sent a recommendation to the UN General Assembly to proclaim a Decade of Disabled Persons – from 1983 to 1992 – to implement the World Program of Action. DPI hoped that during the Decade UN member-countries would make progress in prevention and rehabilitation, and provide resources both for these activities and for the support of organizations of disabled people. Furthermore, they were to consult organizations of disabled people over the implementation of these measures. DPI then did three things to urge the UN to allocate more resources to make the world more aware of the Decade. First, it became involved in exploring a Global Initiative in Support of the Decade, along with IMPACT (International Initiative Against Avoidable Disablement) and ICOD (the International Council on Disability), the latter being a coalition of disability professionals and some uni-disability groups. This planned Global Project, as it came to be called, was planned to span a one-year period, topped off with an international television production. The whole initiative was to be run with funds from business corporations and under the banner of the UN, with its support. The whole point of the Project was to tell the world that this was the Decade of Disabled Persons, with goals needing to be met.

DPI was approached by IMPACT to become involved, but it wondered whether this was the kind of event in which it wanted to be involved. The television production could turn out like a telethon, talking about disabled people either as superstars who are doing so well because they are doing normal things like everyone else, or as pitiable charity cases to whom the public should donate money. DPI decided to be involved so that the principles of full participation, integration and disabled people taking control of their lives would be emphasized; and that the three facets of the WPA — prevention, rehabilitation and equalization of opportunities — would be appropriately represented. Overall, DPI felt that the TV production would have disabled people participating as entertainers and the focus would be on their talents rather than on their disability. It was estimated that the Project would raise a minimum of $50 million (US) to help implement the principles of the WPA.[21] And in the end, most important for DPI, the Decade and the concerns of disabled people would be aired internationally.

At the same time, at regional DPI meetings held during 1987, the midpoint of the Decade, members discovered that governments had done little to implement the WPA in its first half. At these meetings consisting of DPI and representatives of the UN and other non-governmental organizations, it was discovered that many countries had not even recognized the Decade of Disabled Persons, and a DPI questionnaire mailed to its members showed that there was dissatisfaction with the inaction concerning the Decade shown by the UN and by governments.[22]

DPI's concerns about the lack of action culminated in its third battle-plan for recognition of the Decade – launching a lobby effort at the UN General Assembly. In August 1987, in Stockholm, the UN held a Global Meeting of Experts to evaluate the Decade's progress at its midpoint. Over one-third of the Experts chosen by the UN were from DPI member-organizations, and the Chairperson and four out of the five vice-chairpersons were from DPI. As a result, DPI had great influence at the meeting, and most of its recommendations were accepted. It was agreed that there should be more UN publicity about the Decade, and that more resources should be allocated to this. But while DPI wanted only organizations of disabled people to receive funds from the UN Voluntary Fund for the Decade, this was not passed. The Experts' report was to be presented to the UN General Assembly in its October 1987 session. And DPI representatives were at the UN to lobby for adoption of a resolution for governments to strengthen their support for the Decade and the principles of the WPA.

As Henry Enns recalled afterwards, disabled people "stormed the UN".[23] A dozen DPI representatives, with a resolution in hand calling for greater recognition of the Decade, entered the Third Committee of the UN General Assembly (one of five UN General Assembly Committees; the Third is the Social, Humanitarian and Cultural Committee). Knowing that the visitor's gallery for the large meeting room was inaccessible, they proceeded – in wheelchairs, on crutches, with white canes in hand – on to the main floor of the Third Committee, where observers were not allowed. The Clerk of the meeting, perturbed by the seeming pandemonium created by these disabled people, rushed to find the person in charge. He stopped before a person who did not appear to have a disability, and asked if she was in charge of the group, to which she replied, "No," and pointed to Henry Enns in his wheelchair. Then, as Enns recalled, "he turned white as a sheet and was speechless. All the UN rules and regulations had not prepared him for this dilemma. Observers to the UN chambers were only allowed up on the balconies, but the balconies were not accessible. What was he to do with these people in wheelchairs?"[24]

In the end, when government representatives began to approach the DPI representatives to discover why they were there, the Clerk resigned himself to the fact that under the circumstances he could not ask them to leave. Thus, over a three-day period, while the Decade of Disabled Persons was under discussion, several DPI representatives lobbied countries within their region each day. For example, Tambo Camara, a wheelchair-user from Mauritania, was able to speak with delegates from other French-speaking countries.[25]

As a result, a resolution quite similar to DPI's was passed, but unfortunately, because of UN cutbacks, no further UN funds were allocated for the Decade. However, the resolution called on member-governments to contribute more funds to the UN Voluntary Fund for the Decade.[26] But these funds were for local projects, not international publicity about the Decade. It was also agreed at the meeting that the Global Initiative, in which DPI was already involved, would have to fill the funding gap to publicize and implement the principles of the Decade. The Third Committee's resolution was forwarded on to the UN General Assembly and passed in late November 1987.

DPI's lobby effort achieved several things in addition to the adopted resolution. First, it was a training opportunity for DPI representatives who had not lobbied at the UN level before – which happened to be most of the members. Enns, who had attended many UN meetings, provided some advice to the others in the lobbying effort, thus sharing knowledge and expertise that the others could employ at other UN forums, especially at the regional level. An additional benefit to DPI was increased credibility. Several UN officers and representatives of other non-governmental organizations made the observation that DPI had become more sophisticated regarding international matters. They had a sense that DPI knew what it wanted and had itself reasonably well-organized. Enns reported that Hans Hoegh, the Secretary General of the International League of the Red Cross, "commented that he was tremendously impressed by the development and sophistication within DPI during the last few years."[27]

At the next sitting of the Third Committee in 1988, more governments spoke in support of the Decade, and some contributed funds towards its implementation. There was also discussion of, and support for, an "End of Decade conference" to be held in 1992. In addition, many of the UN bodies, such as the WHO and the UNDP, began to allocate funds for disabled persons through various projects in 1988. Indeed, DPI's 1987 lobbying effort appeared to be a turning-point for recognition of the Decade — DPI had educated many countries about the concerns of disabled persons.

Human rights at the United Nations. DPI also gained international recognition at the UN Human Rights Sub-Commission. But most important, the Nazis' killing campaign against disabled people, the devastation to disabled people caused by the economic policies of the US administration under President Reagan, and the beatings of disabled people in Japanese institutions were revealed, and some preventive measures have been taken by the Japanese government as a result of DPI's efforts. The Sub-Commission was part of ECOSOC, and thus DPI used its consultative status to make representations, which reiterated that disabled people should be protected like all other human beings. Ultimately, due to DPI's work, violations against disabled individuals were no longer hidden from public view, and the Sub-Commission became a forum for disability issues where it had not been before.[28] In the end, a Special Rapporteur, or reporter, was appointed to collect data on the human rights violations against people with disabilities in different countries.

DPI representations at the Sub-Commission began indirectly in August, 1982. Disabled people in the United States had issued the report *Trust Betrayed, Hope Denied*, revealing the human rights violations against disabled people that the US Administration was allowing. Reagan's cut-backs in health and social services left many disabled persons living in the community in poverty, and disabled people in institutions lived in crowded, unsanitary conditions. The report, developed by disabled people and human rights attorneys in the United States, was published in cooperation with DPI North America. These people presented the report in August 1982, at the UN Sub-Commission on Prevention of Discrimination and Protection of Minorities; this was a body of human rights experts, not representatives of countries. This Sub-Commission reports to the Human Rights Commission, which accepts or rejects resolutions for action. The Commission then reports to ECOSOC, and ECOSOC reports to the UN General Assembly with the findings.[29]

Bruce Curtis, an American disabled activist who had been involved in the US independent living movement, recalled that throughout history disabled people have

been killed at birth, denied education, denied the right to vote, denied the right to employment, denied the right to marry, denied the right to have families, have been sterilized, scientifically experimented upon and imprisoned in institutions under the most inhuman conditions. We are traditionally the last to receive the benefits or the attention of most societies.[30]

He further related that disabled persons had been exterminated with Jews, gypsies and intellectuals by the Nazis in the Second World War. In the end, the Sub-Commission passed a resolution affirming that disabled people were included under the Universal Declaration of Human Rights, even though they were not explicitly mentioned in the document, and it affirmed that the Sub-Commission would promote the rights of disabled persons.[31]

In 1983 DPI was officially represented at the Sub-Commission hearings by two American attorneys, Jim Donald, a wheelchair-user, and Karen Parker, a nondisabled person. At this meeting, DPI provided evidence of punishments such as amputations and blinding practised by some countries in the Middle East and parts of Asia for crimes such as theft. They asserted in their statements that maiming or disabling the human body in any way was a violation of a person's rights.

By 1984 members of the Sub-Commission had moved from its position of thinking that the Human Rights Sub-Commission was not the appropriate forum to air disability issues, to appointing a Special Rapporteur to look into disability and human rights violations. Indeed, the Sub-Commission realized that disability was interconnected with many issues such as food scarcity, refugees and indigenous people.[32] In its resolution of August 29, 1984, it appointed Leandro Despouy (Argentina) as Special Rapporteur; he was endorsed by DPI since he had demonstrated a sensitivity to disabled people's issues and was an expert on human rights law. The Sub-Commission recommended that his report contain information and recommendations on:

a. Human rights and humanitarian law violations that result in disability or have a particular impact on disabled persons; *b*. Apartheid, as it relates to disability; *c*. All forms of discrimination against disabled persons; *d*. Institutionalization and institutional abuse; *e*. Economic, social and cultural rights as they relate to disability.[33]

The Sub-Commission also asked the Special Rapporteur to pay particular attention to the views of disabled people's organizations. The UN provided the Rapporteur with a salary, but he did not receive funds for expenses for researching a report. Thus DPI has helped the Rapporteur to travel to various DPI meetings to meet disabled people and hear about violations that have occurred in their countries. Originally, Despouy was to report his findings in 1986, but because of the great volume of material that had to be collected, the report was rescheduled to appear in 1988.

DPI has been pleased with the job done by Despouy, as he has been open to consulting with organizations of disabled people. It presented some of the violations that its members had brought to light at the June 1985 Sub-Commission meeting. It cited institutionalization as

cruel, inhuman and degrading treatment. Institutionalization itself causes disabilities, in particular the institutionalized personality, which renders a person inadaptable or less adaptable to normal life in society. The phenomena [*sic*] of the institutionalized personality makes it difficult to diagnose and provide treatment for naturally caused disabilities – often the unnaturally caused personality is assumed to be part of the original disability. Hospitalization of disabled persons is only warranted when disabled persons need acute medical care and actually receive amelioriative acute medical care in the facility of internment.[34]

DPI believed that no person should be institutionalized because it was like being imprisoned for life. It contended that independent living in the community should be encouraged everywhere – in both the developed and developing worlds. But in fact institutionalization was more of a problem in the developed world, where there was money to maintain big institutions. In the developing world, for the most part, there was little money for institutions, and disabled people therefore lived in their communities. Many of those who lived in institutions experienced beatings and sexual assault, and were prescribed drugs to keep them passive and easier to control in an institutional setting. DPI considered such treatment as torture, and inhuman and degrading treatment.

DPI had presented a separate report to the Sub-Commission on alleged beatings and neglect committed against mentally ill persons in several Japanese institutions. Jim Donald, as DPI Human Rights Committee chairperson, investigated the situation in Japan in April 1985. It was found that at one Japanese institution, with a population of 944 inmates in 1984, fifty-eight people died in 1981, seventy-nine in 1982, seventy-four in 1983, and eleven in 1984.[35] In addition, the fact-finding mission discovered that institutions for the mentally ill were privately-run and therefore needed to show a profit. Thus there was often overcrowding and drugging to control patients, reducing them to a state where less staff were needed. DPI urged the need for deinstitutionalization of disabled people, and noted Japan's negligible effort to provide community alternatives.[36]

Largely as a result of DPI's efforts, Japan passed a new mental health act in the fall of 1987 to address some of the uncovered abuses. While the legislation did not address all the problems, it was a first step, and DPI hoped ''that other nations might study this case as an example of how this forum [the UN Commission on Human Rights] can lead to favorable results for both victims and governments.''[37] DPI planned to continue monitoring the application of the Japanese legislation, especially the deinstitutionalization process that was to be initiated. This was a victory for disabled people's human rights everywhere. As the DPI Human Rights Committee explained, ''Some governments, concerned that we might take up the situation in their countries, quietly began a reform process. (We are informed, for instance, that the USSR is modifying its mental health laws.)''[38]

Finally, DPI was concerned with humanitarian law violations that caused disabilities in the world. It cited war and armed conflict as prime disablers of people, calling for peace and for countries to redirect their wealth away from the crippling of humankind toward instruments of life.[39]

Peace issues

DPI has addressed peace issues, as they relate to disability, since its founding in 1981. At its First World Congress, it called for 1 per cent of all money spent on the arms race to be redirected to useful projects that promote life, such as clean water and food.

DPI deplored the waste of human life and the disabling effects of war, as it declared in its "Peace Statement" in Hiroshima, Japan, which it drafted in June 1982 when its World Council met in Tokyo. The members then travelled to Hiroshima, and participated in a peace march with people disabled in the atom bomb blast in 1945. The "Peace Statement" asserted:

Disabled People all over the world know, from their deepest personal experience, the capacity of war to cast its mantle of death and destruction over life and limb . . . "[40]

It further insisted that "the 600 billion now spent a year on armaments is diverted to socially useful projects."[41]

Generally, DPI's World Council members were in agreement about calling for peace. But in Hiroshima, when some World Council members drew up a peace petition that they wanted DPI to distribute worldwide, some World Council members were reluctant to cooperate in circulating it. They claimed that such a petition would not be well-received by their governments or people.

DPI decided that it would embark on a "DPI Ship of Peace" project in 1986, the International Year of Peace. The Brotherhood of Man, an international sailing organization for disabled people, approached DPI with a proposal for a Ship of Peace that would sail around the world crewed totally by disabled people. It was to be DPI-sponsored and would stop at the UN in New York and at Hiroshima on its world tour. The plan was for twenty-eight disabled people to sail from Sweden, leaving in September 1986, but the project was cancelled due to funding complications. Originally, the Swedish government and a pharmaceutical company were to be the ship's sponsors, but because of conflicts between the scheme's main organizer and the pharmaceutical company, the pharmaceutical funder withdrew from the project. DPI then decided that the ship was not its major priority to fund in 1986 because its Development Program and internal operations needed funding.[42] This ship project may yet be embarked upon in the future if funds become available.

In addition to DPI's peace efforts, there was a local peace initiative undertaken by the Movement of the Lebanese Handicapped in Defence of Human Rights in Lebanon. In October 1987, a group of fifty disabled people – wheelchair and crutch users – marched across Lebanon calling for both sides to put aside their differences. Their group was non-sectarian, not for the Christians nor for the Muslims, but for all Lebanese. It had been founded in August 1985 to protest against the Lebanese civil war, as they "recognized themselves as symbolic of today's Lebanon – crippled by chaotic turmoil, succeeding only in proliferating the proportion of handicapped people in the country."[43] Almost immediately, the group's twenty-seven disabled members demonstrated against the war in the streets of war-torn Beirut. This was a test run of the larger, potentially more dangerous march across Lebanon, which would cross the line in Beirut separating the warring Christian and Muslim factions, and end up in Tyre. Before embarking on this longer trip the group solicited the moral support of DPI and groups such as the British Council of Organizations of Disabled People, Oxfam and the Arab Organization for Human Rights. In Britain, disabled people marched on October 15, 1987, in solidarity with the Lebanese.

In Lebanon, the disabled people marched for six days, from October 12 to 17, and covered 190 kilometers. When they reached Beirut they planted white flags in bombed out areas. Most of the marchers, like Toufic Alloush and George Bardaweel, had been disabled by the war, as reported by the Associated Press:

George Bardaweel, a Christian, had worked as a Civil Defense rescuer. He lost his left leg when a mortar round slammed into his ambulance during a rescue mission in West Beirut in 1984. 'I still work as a private nurse, but certainly not a rescuer,' Bardaweel said in an interview . . .

Alloush, a Sunni Muslim, was caught in the crossfire of a clash between rival militiamen in the northern city of Tripoli in 1983. 'I was hit by three bullets in the back, one of them shattered the spinal cord and I've been crippled from the waist down," said Alloush, a basketball trainer.[44]

Striving for peace remained on the agendas of many disabled people and of DPI.

DPI and the International Labor Organization

Around the world some disabled people are working, in menial jobs, for one dollar (US) a day, and unemployment of disabled people varies, according to the country in question, from 60 to 99 per cent. For this reason DPI has also affirmed that employment is the right of every human being. Bengt Lindqvist summed up this concern:

"Everybody must feel they have something to offer to others. To have a job or a meaningful role, to feel that one contributes to one's family and to one's society, is the right of every individual."[45] Thus, with this philosophy, DPI set out to influence the policies of the ILO, the major international organization dealing with employment issues. It was placed on the ILO's Special List, a kind of consultative status, on May 21, 1984, and could thus express its views on employment matters as they related to disabled people and the ILO.[46] As a result, many of DPI's views were incorporated into the ILO's "Vocational Rehabilitation (Disabled Persons) Convention and Recommendation". The Convention called for the promotion of employment opportunities for disabled people in the integrated labor market, and the Recommendation set out a "series of suggested measures aimed at increasing employment opportunities for disabled persons such as assistance and financial incentives to employers to encourage them to provide training and employment for disabled persons and to make adaptation to workplaces. . . ."[47] In this process DPI again debated over the definitions of "impairment", "disability", and "handicap".

The issue of employment is important for everyone in society. Being a worker is a valued role, and is associated with the status of adulthood. Production, the direct result of work, is of course also highly valued. If people do not work, how do they adequately feed and clothe themselves and their families? Thus employment in the mainstream of the community, like anyone else, is important to disabled people both for self-esteem and for self-support.

In the nineteenth century, disabled individuals were often beggars or laborers in workhouses, and many post-1945 sheltered workshops were similar to workhouses; they exploited disabled people's labor. Disabled people often did such menial tasks as rolling up posters or packaging thumbtacks for $.50 to $1.00 (US) per day. This was often called vocational rehabilitation of disabled people, but these workshops often have not provided training in marketable job skills to enable those working there to move out into the mainstream workforce. Thus many disabled people would work and "train" there for many years. Many disabled people and their organizations began to speak out against this form of employment. Furthermore, disabled people have pushed to be integrated into the mainstream of the employment arena, where the vast majority of them have not worked. In the United States, in 1984, 27.4 per cent of people with disabilities worked,[48] and, correspondingly, more than 70 per cent were unemployed and living on social assistance, with the result that many unemployed disabled people lived in poverty. The attitudes of society have handicapped their efforts to enter the workforce. Often the assumption is that if persons could not walk, they also could not talk, see or even think. Disabled people have been seen as totally incapacitated.

DPI asserted that employers needed to be educated about the abilities of disabled people. They also needed to be educated about "reasonable accommodation". Many worksites were initially inaccessible to disabled people, who therefore could not work there. For example, a wheelchair-user who was a draughtsperson might not be able to work at a regular drawing board because it was too high. The employer could reasonably accommodate the person for a low cost by lowering the board to a level suitable for the person's height. Workplace modifications enabled disabled people to work like anyone else. Thus DPI viewed the ILO Vocational Rehabilitation and Employment discussions as an opportunity to convey disabled persons' concerns about their unemployment and underemployment.

The ILO has a tripartate consultative system with governments, workers and employers represented in country delegations, on whom the ILO Convention is binding if they agree to it. When one is to be passed, the countries belonging to the ILO take it back home to have their government, workers and employers ratify it. Once a Convention has been ratified, a country is bound to implement it, and reports back to the ILO periodically on progress with its implementation. A Recommendation, on the other hand, is more informal, since it only suggests guidelines that countries can follow.

DPI worked on the ILO Vocational Rehabilitation issue with governments and other international disability organizations, and they met in Paris in April 1983 before the second ILO meeting dealing with the Vocational Rehabilitation issue. The organizations comprised Rehabilitation International, the International Federation of the Blind, the International League of Societies for Persons with Mental Handicap, the World Council for the Welfare of the Blind, and DPI. They agreed that a "convention" and not merely a "recommendation", should be pursued at the ILO meeting in June. A convention was wanted because it would be binding and thus more effective in enacting changes in vocational rehabilitation, training and employment of disabled persons.[49] They knew, however, that because it usually took three years of sittings of the vocational rehabilitation committee to obtain a convention, their chances of doing so at that late date were slim. Furthermore, the vocational rehabilitation policy to be discussed in June 1983 was already in the form of a recommendation, and it would probably be accepted at this meeting.

DPI went into the meeting pushing for the participation of disabled people in vocational rehabilitation policy planning and implementation. It wanted this recognized in any ILO mechanism, just as it had insisted that the World Program of Action should recognize the importance of disabled people's organizations having input on policies that affected disabled people. Already, in 1982, the Canadian government had recommended that disabled people should be consulted and that representatives of their organizations should be invited to the next meeting in 1983,[50] and indeed international organizations such as DPI and the International Federation of the Blind did attend this meeting. Technically, observers could speak only if they were backed by workers or employers at the meeting, and DPI was almost denied the right to speak because the employers made a move to block its participation.

It was a controversy over definitions that alienated the employers from DPI. The employers were sure that disabled people would support a definition of "disabled persons" as those who were recognized as disabled by an expert – in other words, by a professional. DPI disagreed with this definition, contending that only a disabled person could define whether he or she was disabled or not. Furthermore, DPI did not accept the WHO's definition, which viewed "handicap" as the problem of the individual, which was to be included in the ILO policy. The US employers' representative then put forth a motion at the meeting to deny DPI speaking privileges. This caused a furor: the workers and a number of governments were upset because the majority of participants wanted to hear disabled people's views on employment issues that affected them. This incident elevated DPI's profile as the legitimate voice of disabled people.

Three issues were debated at the meeting. The definition, as already mentioned, was hotly debated. DPI wanted "handicap" to be defined as a function of the relationship between the disabled person and his or her environment. This definition was not adopted, and instead a compromise was reached whereby a "disabled" person meant "an individual whose prospects of securing, retaining and advancing in suitable employment are substantially reduced as a result of a duly recognized physical or mental impairment."[51] The term "duly recognized" inferred that a professional person could define whether a person was disabled or not, with which DPI still disagreed.

The second issue that DPI pressed for was the participation of disabled people and their organizations in vocational rehabilitation planning and implementation. DPI – again through its representatives Henry Enns, Ron Chandran-Dudley, DPI chairperson, and Jan Johnsson, head of secretariat – lobbied the delegations for support. Ultimately, a clause calling for the participation of disabled people's organizations was included in the resulting Recommendation, which was a set of guidelines and principles – not binding – for countries to follow.

The third issue debated was whether to adopt a convention, and the Swedish and Canadian workers' representatives were the prime movers. The Swedish workers introduced an amendment proposing that a convention be written and adopted, supplemented with a recommendation. Ultimately, a convention was accepted with 343 for, none against and 77 abstentions.[52]

So the ILO member-countries had to take the Convention back home, as already mentioned, to consult with their governments, with workers and with employers to have it ratified. In the end, it could be defeated by a government's legislative body and ratification would not be obtained. Organizations of disabled persons have thus actively lobbied their governments to accept the Convention. It became effective on June 20, 1985, and by November 1988 had been ratified by twenty-three countries.[53]

Thus, DPI has had some impact on international policies through lobbying at international forums. Whether these policies themselves will have any impact will only be known in the future, but DPI used the available international policy-making meetings to work towards change.

NOTES

1   DPI, "DPI Pamphlet", 1980, 1.
2   Virginia F. Saurwein, chief of unit, Non-Governmental Organizations Unit, Dept. of International Economic and Social Affairs, to Henry Enns, May 16, 1983, DPI Development Office files, Winnipeg.
3   DPI, "Application for Consultative Status with ECOSOC", May 1982, DPI Development Office files, Winnipeg.
4   Ron Chandran-Dudley and Henry Enns, "UN Report", Winnipeg, 1983, 2, DPI Development Office files, Winnipeg.
5   *Ibid.*, 3.
6   Amadou-Mahtar M'Bow, director-general of UNESCO, to Ron Chandran-Dudley, DPI chairperson, Aug. 6, 1985.*
7   Telephone interview with Jan Johnsson, head of Secretariat, DPI, Jan. 20, 1988.
8   *Ibid.*, July 23, 1986, and Jan. 20, 1988.

9   Gunnel Nelson, World Health Organization (WHO), "Community-based Rehabilitation", "DPI Seminar, Turku, Finland, Aug. 21-4, 1983, Report", Stockholm, 2, DPI Development Office files, Winnipeg.

10   *Ibid.*, 1.

11   *Ibid.*

12   DPI, "Report From Drafting Committee 1983-08-24", in "DPI Turku Seminar Report", 8.

13   Henry Enns, "Background to World Program of Action", Winnipeg, *ca.* 1984, 1, DPI Development Office files, Winnipeg.

14   Henry Enns, "International Disability Issues: Canadian Involvement", Winnipeg, March 1985, 6, Henry Enns files, Winnipeg.

15   Henry Enns, "World Program of Action Analysis", Winnipeg, *ca.* 1983, 1, DPI Development Office files, Winnipeg.

16   *Ibid.*, 1-2.

17   United Nations, *World Program of Action Concerning Disabled Persons* (New York: United Nations, 1983), 8.

18   Henry Enns and Bengt Lindqvist, "Report on United Nations Advisory Committee", *ca.* 1982, Winnipeg, 1, DPI Development Office files, Winnipeg.

19   Vic Finkelstein, "World Health Organization Meeting, June 24-28, 1985, Netherlands", *British Council of Organizations of Disabled People Newsletter*, 3 (Jan. 1986), 10.

20   Telephone interview with André LeBlanc, former director, Bureau on Rehabilitation, Health and Welfare Canada, Ottawa, June 10, 1985.

21   Henry Enns, "Chairperson's Report", Sweden, Aug. 1987, 1, Henry Enns files, Winnipeg.

22   *Ibid.*; DPI North American/Caribbean Region, "UN Decade of Disabled Persons, 1983-1992, North American/Caribbean Region, Mid-Term Evaluation Seminar, 27-8 July, 1987", Kingston, Jamaica, 1-3, Henry Enns files, Winnipeg.

23   Henry Enns, "Disabled People Storm UN Headquarters", *Vox Nostra* (Jan. 1988), 1-2.

24   Enns, "Disabled People Storm", 1.

25   Interview with Paula Keirstead, DPI chief development officer, Winnipeg, Dec. 17, 1987.

26   UN Third Committee, "Implementation of the World Program of Action Concerning Disabled Persons and the United Nations Decade of Disabled Persons, Draft Resolution", 42nd session, Agenda item 93, Oct. 26, 1987.

27   DPI chairperson and the secretariat, "DPI Communiqué", Dec. 1987, 1, Henry Enns files, Winnipeg.

28   Interview with Jim Donald, chairperson, DPI Human Rights Committee, Nassau, Sept. 18, 1985.

29   Henry Enns, "Report on Meeting of Human Rights Sub-Commission, Geneva, May 3-31, 1984", Winnipeg, 1, DPI Development Office files, Winnipeg.

30   Bruce Curtis, "UN Sub-Commission Presentation", Aug. 1982, 1, DPI Development Office files, Winnipeg.

31   Disabled People's Delegation, "Draft Resolution", to Sub-Commission on Prevention of Discrimination and Protection of Minorities, Aug. 1982, DPI Development Office files, Winnipeg.

32   Donald interview.

33   DPI, "Human Rights and Disability: Report of Disabled Peoples' International to

United Nations Sub-Commission on Prevention of Discrimination and Protection of Minorities, 38th Session'', 1985, 2.*

34   *Ibid.*, 12.

35   Etsuro Totsuka, Kantoro Nagano and Junri Ozaki, ''Patient's Rights and Consumer Movement'', presented at 11th IOCU World Congress, Bangkok, Dec. 9–14, 1984, 4.*

36   DPI Human Rights Committee, ''Preliminary Report on the Institutionalized Mentally Ill in Japan'', presented to UN Sub-Commission on Prevention of Discrimination and Protection of Minorities, 38th Session, 1985, 3.*

37   DPI, ''Question of Human Rights of Detainees'', statement to United Nations Economic and Social Council on Human Rights, 44th Session, Agenda item 10, 1988, 1.

38   DPI Human Rights Committee, ''Human Rights Committee Report for 1987/1988'', 2.

39   DPI Human Rights Committee, ''Human Rights and Disability'', 8.

40   DPI ''Peace Statement'', Hiroshima, Japan, June 24, 1982, DPI Development Office files, Winnipeg.

41   *Ibid.*

42   Interview with Henry Enns, Winnipeg, July 31, 1986.

43   Lebanon's Disabled Peace Campaign, ''Synopsis of the Campaign'', April 1987, Henry Enns' files, Winnipeg.

44   ''War Wounded Cross Green Line: Lebanese Christians, Muslims demonstrate for Peace in Beirut'', *Winnipeg Free Press*, Oct. 15, 1987, 20.

45   Bengt Lindqvist, ''The Right to Work: A Political Issue'' in Kathleen S. Miller, Linda M. Chadderdon and Barbara Duncan (*eds*), *Participation of People with Disabilities: An International Perspective* (East Lansing, Michigan: University Center for International Rehabilitation, Michigan State University, 1981), 17.

46   Manuel Carrillo, Liaison Officer for Non-Governmental Organizations, ILO, to Jan Johnsson, Head of DPI Secretariat, May 21, 1984, DPI Development Office files, Winnipeg.

47   Sam Niwa (ILO), ''Presentation to DPI Seminar in Turku'' in ''DPI Seminar, Turku, Finland, August 21–24, 1983, Report'', Stockholm, 1983, DPI Development Office files, Winnipeg.

48   William D. Frey, ''Introduction'' in Rochelle V. Habeck *et al.* (*eds*), *Economics and Equity in Employment of People with Disabilities: International Policies and Practices* (Michigan: University Centre for International Rehabilitation, Michigan State University, 1985), ix.

49   World Council for the Welfare of the Blind, ''Model letter for use by national organizations of and for disabled persons to address their Governments'', April 1983, DPI Development Office files, Winnipeg.

50   Interview with Henry Enns, DPI deputy chairperson, Winnipeg, Sept. 5, 1985.

51   Jane Atkey and André LeBlanc, ''Report on Committee on Vocational Rehabilitation Second Discussion at the ILO Conference, Geneva, June 1983'', July 1983, 4, DPI Development Office files, Winnipeg.

52   *Ibid.*, p. 3.

53   S.I. Niwa, chief, Vocational Rehabilitation Branch Training Dept., ILO, to Diane Driedger, Nov. 18, 1988.*

9

CONCLUSION: ONWARD. . . .

"I sometimes think human society is asleep and dreaming a dream where some people are perfect, beautiful, and powerful and others are flawed, unbeautiful and powerless. In the dream the perfect people play their immortal parts and the imperfect people are rejected from human life. We are helping to awaken humanity to the reality that all people are flawed and yet beautiful, and each one limited in his or her unique way and yet powerful."[1]

— Jim Derksen, DPI, in Dakar, Senegal, 1983

"Let's travel towards the future with enthusiasm and joy, but without childish hastiness."[2]

— Pedro Roberto Cruz (Uruguay), DPI World Council member, 1987

By 1989 nine years of marches, speeches, seminars and lobbying efforts had built DPI nationally and internationally. DPI is the organizational manifestation of the international multi-disability movement. While organizations such as the International Federation of the Blind and the International Federation of the Deaf represented blind and deaf people respectively, DPI spoke for people with various disabilities. Locally and nationally, its existence has spurred disabled people on to organize themselves as they saw disabled people succeeding in other parts of the world.

At international forums, such as the ILO and the United Nations and its bodies, DPI has had an impact on the direction of policies regarding disabled people. It is true that to date these policies may not have had much measurable impact on the lives of disabled people at the grassroots level, but disabled people have participated in the available international forums like other groups of people in the world. And, most important, people of all disability groups have had a voice internationally where there was none before.

This voice has contributed to disabled people's sense of self-esteem. They have learned, as Ed Roberts, a veteran of the US disabled people's movement, has often said: "We are powerful and beautiful." At an international level, disabled people have participated in the Council and in leadership training programs, and have had employment with DPI. In the process they have gained a sense of confidence that they can contribute to society like anyone else. But DPI, being an international voice, also impressed on disabled individuals that they were not alone – other disabled individuals felt like they did and were speaking out. Many disabled people felt pride in this fact. Thus international and national credibility helped them define who they were – they were citizens like all other human beings. They were not charity cases, or the clients and patients of do-gooders, social workers and doctors. Indeed, they defined themselves at UN, ILO, and WHO meetings as being handicapped by the inaccessible social and physical environment that limited their participation.

DPI gained international credibility with the UN, ILO, non-governmental development agencies and some governments, especially Canada and Sweden. It achieved international recognition with the ECOSOC, the ILO and UNESCO within five years of its founding. It has influenced the direction of international policy documents – the World Program of Action Concerning Disabled Persons and the ILO's Vocational Rehabilitation Convention. The question, then, is: how have these accomplishments benefitted disabled people, if they have done so at all? Often international forums can merely be debating societies and not result in much action, and realistically the World Program of Action and the ILO Convention have yet not resulted in changes for grassroots disabled people. But the international respect gained by the disabled people's movement at all levels, and the chance to voice concerns at these international forums, have the potential in the years to come to benefit the average disabled citizen.

International recognition has often led DPI into partnerships with organizations interested in projects which include disabled people. Indeed, international bodies, governments and international development aid agencies have begun learning about disabled people and their needs from disabled persons themselves. A new awareness of the need to include disabled people's concerns in development plans at the UN and in the programming of non-governmental agencies has dawned. The International Year of Disabled Persons (IYDP), coupled with the founding of DPI, both of which were in 1981, brought these concerns to the fore in the 1980s. This meant that an increasing number of non-governmental organizations started to contribute funds to the administration of DPI and its Leadership Training Development Program. From 1980 till 1985, thirteen non-governmental organizations contributed to the activities of DPI, mostly its seminars and congresses. The UN IYDP Trust Fund and the ILO also contributed.[3] But again this has not resulted in overnight independence, economic self-sufficiency and improved quality of life for disabled people worldwide. However, there have been some moves in this direction. DPI's Development Program has had a direct personal impact on at least 600 to 700 disabled people, increasing their self-esteem and their management skills, which can now be used in developing disabled people's organizations and employment opportunities for themselves and others.

Perhaps DPI's greatest impact has been in spurring disabled people on to organize themselves into sixty-nine national multi-disability groups by 1989. The development of disabled persons' groups was a by-product of some of the Leadership Training Seminars, as with Guyana. After the Barbados Training Seminar in 1983, the Guyanese delegates returned to their country and founded an organization of disabled persons. The growth of organizations in all regions was important for disabled people to obtain a voice and a mechanism to pressure governments on changes for disabled people. DPI has aided the credibility of some organizations, particularly in the Caribbean, where Derrick Palmer, the DPI Regional Development Officer, met government officials.

Individual members of the DPI World Council have also begun to gain political influence in their countries. Since DPI's inception in 1980, five members of its Council have become politicians and government cabinet ministers. Bengt Linqvist, who resigned from the World Council in 1986, became the Swedish Minister for Family Affairs and Matters Concerning the Elderly and the Disabled. Philip Goldson, a blind member of the World Council, is the Minister of Local Government, Social Services, Health and Disabled Persons. In Japan, Senator Eita Yashiro, a wheelchair-user and former television entertainer, is the Vice-Minister for Science and Technology. Emanuel Hosein, a physician who is mobility-impaired, became the Minister of Health in Trinidad and Tobago. And, Joshua Malinga, a crutch-user and former businessman, was elected as a city councillor for Bulawayo, Zimbabwe, in 1987. These people have an opportunity to influence policy-making in their countries. And the positions they have achieved are symbolic of the growing influence of disabled people and their organizations, including DPI, which are training future leaders for society. Indeed their involvement points to the potential of all disabled persons to make contributions in the world. With the removal of attitudinal and architectural barriers, and with leadership training and increased self-confidence, disabled individuals will participate more fully in every sphere of life. DPI has been at the forefront of making possible this ever-increasing participation.

DPI will continue in the future to strive for its principles of self-determination, equality, integration and peace. By the end of the 1980s it had many tools – funds, volunteer and paid personnel, international recognition and innovative lobby tactics – at its disposal. How long DPI will be strong on the international scene, foster social change and mean something to its membership will be told as the future unfolds. The struggle for rights was not over. It had only just begun.

NOTES

1   Jim Derksen, "Speech to the DPI Dakar, Senegal Leadership Training Seminar", Dec. 7–15, 1982, Dakar, Senegal, 5, DPI Development Office files, Winnipeg.
2   Pedro Roberto Cruz, "The General Struggle and the Participation of the Disabled", *Vox Nostra* (Jan. 1988), 9.
3   DPI, "List of Donations and Grants to DPI (Canada) Inc., 1980–85", DPI Development Office files, Winnipeg.

10

EPILOGUE: DISABLED PEOPLES' INTERNATIONAL AND SOCIAL MOVEMENT THEORY

While Disabled People's International (DPI) has made its own unique stamp on history, it has features in common with other social movements. Originally, my thesis on DPI included the social movement theory of sociologist Armand L. Mauss as an indicator of how DPI had developed as a movement and where it may be headed. Realizing that some readers may not be that interested in theoretical interjections in each chapter, I decided to include them in an appendix consolidating the theory into one essay.

This essay reviews several social movement theorists and concludes with the theory of Armand L. Mauss, whose stages of movement development serve as the best indicator about the fate of DPI's future as a social movement organization. However, this is not a formal testing of Mauss's theory to discover where it fits DPI and where it does not.

First, Ralph Turner explains the reasons for the development of a social movement concerned with bringing about change:

A significant social movement becomes possible when there is a revision in the manner in which a substantial group of people, looking at some misfortune, sees it no longer as a misfortune warranting charitable consideration but as an injustice which is intolerable to society.[4]

Thus, a movement is formed when a group of people stop petitioning others for relief of their conditions and instead demand amelioration of conditions as a right.

In addition, Zurcher and Snow examine the membership and organization of social movements.[5] Most important, they discuss the process of movements becoming organizations: "Organization is necessary if a movement is to make any headway in its goal-attainment efforts."[6] They go on, though, to state that organization can lead to acquiescence and thus frustrate the attainment of goals. They conclude that "the problem is not organization *per se*, but organizations that fail to develop and maintain a sense of enthusiasm and anticipation."[7] Thus, organization does not work against social movement goals, but organization without passion leads to stagnation. A dialectical tension between enthusiasm and idealism on one hand, and bureaucratism and pragmatism on the other is present.

Turner and Killian, on the other hand, discuss the life cycle of social movements. They explain that "the life cycle is a way of organizing our knowledge about movements so as to permit prediction of forthcoming events."[8] Indeed, this model can be useful in analyzing the organizational life of DPI. The authors provide four stages of development. In the first there is general and unfocussed unrest in a population. In the second stage the reasons for unrest are focussed toward what should be changed. In the third stage, called "formal organization", the movement becomes a disciplined organization with goals and strategies. Finally, in the "institutional stage", the movement becomes an organic part of society.

While Zurcher and Snow, and Turner and Killian, prove helpful in considering DPI's development, the work of Armand Mauss is the most useful. First, he discusses how society defines reality and social problems, and holds that there is a consensual reality, or set of beliefs, on which most people in society can agree. But when those beliefs fall short of fulfilling the expectations of different interest groups, "social problems" are defined:

When, however, this consensual reality, or common stock of knowledge, fails to 'deliver the goods', or to make possible the solution of everyday problems, then people will begin to question it and will be open to new constructions of reality being offered by special interest groups.[9]

Mauss then explains that social movements or interest groups arise and redefine a situation in society as a social problem. The movement then influences the public's view of reality. According to Mauss, there are two types of consensual reality, informal and formal. Informal consensual reality is found in folklore, myths and anecdotes: it is a truth that is commonly understood in society, such as the idea that the growth of youth violence in society is an example of the loss of respect of youth for property and their elders. But in the case of disabled people, Mauss' concept of formal consensual reality is most important to consider.

Formal consensual reality is defined by organizations, institutions or people who are considered as authorities. Examples of formal consensual reality are scientific and statistical studies. In the case of disabled people, this would be the reality proposed by medical and social work professionals – the experts on disability. The public generally believes in the truth of their pronouncements because they hold the truth through scientific and medical rehabilitation knowledge. The disabled people's movement questioned these professionals' definition of reality for them; this was the "medical model", which holds that disabled people are sick and must spend their whole lives getting well. Disabled people began to reject this medical definition of themselves after the Second World War. They started to define themselves as citizens of the world with the same rights as everyone else. It was not their fault that they could not climb stairs or read print; it was the inaccessible environment erected by society that handicapped them. Thus, in the post-1945 world disabled people set out to redefine their situation for medical and social work professionals and the public. This redefinition process played an important role in DPI right from its beginnings. In 1980, at the Rehabilitation International (RI) World Congress, disabled people defined themselves as citizens with rights: they believed that they were not the patients and caseloads of doctors and social workers. Redefinition was also important in DPI's lobby efforts at the ILO and at meetings concerning the World Program of Action Concerning Disabled Persons (WPA). In both cases, DPI asserted that "handicap" must be defined as societal barriers that handicap them, not as a problem on the individual's side. The definition question has been of great importance to DPI, because if you cannot define who you are on your own, and have society accept it, society will attempt to control you through its definitions, in this case the medical model.

Mauss also discusses factors that cause people to create and join social movements. A group that society defines as "subordinate" finds itself in a position where it has "rising expectations". It compares what it has to what others have in terms of money, status, power or possessions, and believes that it is also entitled to have those things. Thus, when a group's rising expectations are frustrated by society, the group experiences "relative deprivation". According to Mauss, there are five kinds of relative deprivation: economic, social, ethical, physical and psychological. Mauss emphasizes that "it is important to remember that his/her [the "subordinate" member's] 'deprivation' in any case is defined by his/her own perceptions and is likely to be relative to time, place and situation."[10] Disabled people, having become more physically mobile, better educated and more independent after the Second World War, believed that they were citizens with the same rights as everyone else in society.

Because disabled people believed they should be partners in planning policies that affected their lives, they rejected participation in RI. They then formed their own social movement, DPI, to address their feelings of relative deprivation. This concept arose again when deaf people and women both expressed their frustrated expectations of equal participation in DPI. They perceived that they did not have as much power in decision-making as other groups of disabled people in DPI. In particular, at the Bahamas World Congress in 1985, the women threatened to form their own social movement in the face of their experience of relative deprivation.

Mauss also outlines the concept of "resource management" which movements use to mobilize successfully for change. Two of the most important resources are the leadership and the membership. If these two become successfully mobilized for action, there will be committed volunteers to build the movement. Indeed, the initial leadership efforts of the Steering Committee were essential to the mobilization of disabled people to form DPI. Early on in its development, committed leaders and membership have meant successful building of national organizations all over the world and a fervor for furthering DPI's rights-oriented philosophy. Other important resources in mobilization are ideology and strategies and tactics. The ideology or philosophy of the movement must be such as to appeal to the members: "These beliefs must be capable of providing a satisfactory explanation to members and prospective members concerning the causes of the problem and the steps that must be taken to solve it."[11] In addition, strategies (the movement's plans) and tactics (the means of carrying out the plans) are important to social movements: ". . . mobilization involves a repertory of successful strategies and tactics, which will help build membership, influence politicians or raise money."[12] The kinds of tactics movements employ are lobbying, fund-raising, seeking alliances and speaking in the media.

DPI has employed these tactics successfully throughout its short life. The break with Rehabilitation International in Winnipeg in 1980 is a good example of its adeptness. It mobilized the media through the CBC "Summerscope" program filming COPOH delegates and through the on-site *Newsline* enabling disabled delegates to communicate. DPI's lobbying tactics worked well at the meetings to draft the UN World Program of Action and at the UN General Assembly where disabled people marched in and lobbied government representatives. Thus in most cases DPI successfully mobilized its leadership, membership, strategies and tactics, philosophy and funds to foster changes for disabled people. However, conflicts in the World Council and some administrative mismanagement meant that at times resources were not used to their full potential for the movement.

Mauss discusses the leadership needed at different stages in social movements. He claims that the leadership of most movements comes from the middle class and from people in professions where freedom of speech is generally accepted, e.g. teachers, lawyers, writers and other intellectuals. He discusses different kinds of leadership: charismatic, rational-legal and traditional. Charismatic leaders usually inspire and theorize for a movement in its beginning stages. Rational-legal leaders are usually salaried staff and people in positions in the hierarchy of the formal organization.[13] Traditional leadership is the handing down of power and position through the generations, of which the succession of kings and queens is an obvious example. Traditional leadership is not generally relevant for social movements because it takes time to develop and most social movements are short-lived.[14]

Armand Mauss' social movement life-cycle and the development of leadership provides many insights into DPI's development. The first stage of movements, according to Mauss, is "incipiency". This stage is characterized by uncoordinated, unorganized efforts for change with no established membership or leadership. At this stage, the movement is a concerned public. The protest efforts of disabled people at the Rehabilitation International (RI) Congresses in 1972 and 1976 were the reactions of a concerned disabled public. They did not formally organize themselves for action at this point. Furthermore, RI tried to placate their concerns and demands for participation by establishing an *ad hoc* committee on participation. RI's efforts were a symptom of this stage: "Rather than generate conflict, most of the institutions and agencies of the society will attempt a restoration of the consensus through conciliation, compromise and absorption."[15]

The international multi-disability movement quickly moved to the "coalescence stage" when RI failed to meet disabled people's demands for equal participation right away. Disabled people believed equal participation in the decision-making bodies of RI was their right, and at the Winnipeg Congress they reacted against RI, which they perceived was oppressing them. Mauss' life-cycle explains that in this stage people will initiate *ad hoc* groups to formalize their demands for change, which will be formed

in response to repressive and provocative acts on the parts of the government or of other institutions of the "establishment"; it may also occur as the result of disappointment from perceived failures of the government or society to take ameliorative action after raising general hopes and expectations that such would be forthcoming.[16]

RI disappointed disabled people's hopes of equal decision-making power in 1980. Thus disabled persons formed an *ad hoc* Steering Committee to formalize an organization as a vehicle for its demands. Furthermore, the leadership in this stage was charismatic. The people elected to the Steering Committee were seen as possessing the vision disabled people in Winnipeg wanted. Charismatic leadership continued to be influential in the next stage as well.

DPI was formed in 1981, and then moved on to the "institutionalization" or peak stage of a social movement. Mauss explains this stage:

Institutionalization in this sense is accompanied by all the characteristics of a 'full-blown' movement: society-wide organization and coordination (unless the movement happens to deal with strictly local issues); a large base of members and resources; an extended division of labor; regular thrusts into the political processes of the society (e.g. lobbying, campaigning in elections); and growing respectibility.[17]

In this stage the movement has its greatest success through media exposure. Legislation begins to be passed to ameliorate the problems identified by the movement. The leadership can now be of two types, charismatic and rational-legal. DPI retained from its initial Steering Committee stage many of its charismatic leaders who still provided the philosophical base for the organization. Rational-legal leadership was introduced into the organization when full-time staff people were employed in the DPI Secretariat and Development Office.

DPI had entered the institutional stage after its Singapore Congress in 1981. By the time of its Second World Congress in 1985, it had respectibility in the eyes of the UN system, international development aid agencies and some governments. It influenced the "legislation" at international forums – the ILO's Convention and the UN World Program of Action Concerning Disabled Persons. Governments, UN and development aid agencies granted money for DPI activities.

It will be interesting to observe how DPI, the manifestation of the international movement of disabled people, will develop in future. According to Mauss' life cycle, the very success of a movement leads to "fragmentation" and eventual "demise". In the fragmentation stage many movement followers are lost through their "cooptation" into society at large. This also happens when their social situation improves somewhat, and many of the followers believe " 'things have really improved' and that the threat to their vital interests has greatly subsided."[18] At this same stage the leaders, who remain in the movement, will begin fighting among themselves about strategy and tactics for the future. Finally the movement will die out. This does not mean that all the problems have been solved, but rather it is a cleaning-up phase for society: "The cooptation process has appropriated the most critical elements of the movement's program, has 'bought off' many of its leaders . . ."[19] Thus the cycle of a social movement is ended. But social movements, including DPI, leave a legacy in normative and legal changes.[20] Indeed, people with disabilities within DPI hope that the world will have finally ceased to view them as helpless cripples, and begin to accept them as citizens with rights.

NOTES

1   Ralph H. Turner, "The Theme of Contemporary Social Movements", *British Journal of Sociology* (Dec. 1969), 391.

2   Louis A. Zurcher and David A. Snow, "Collective Behavior: Social Movements", in Morris Rosenberg and Ralph H. Turner (*eds*), *Social Psychology: Sociological Perspectives* (New York: Basic Books, 1981), 447–82.

3   *Ibid.*, 478.

4   *Ibid.*

5   Ralph H. Turner and Lewis M. Killian, *Collective Behavior*, 2nd edn (Englewood Cliffs, NJ: Prentice-Hall, 1972), 253.

6   Armand L. Mauss, *Social Problems as Social Movements* (Philadelphia: J.B. Lippincott, 1975), 8.

7   *Ibid.*, 17.

8   *Ibid.*, 56.

9   *Ibid.*

10   *Ibid.*, 52–5.

11   *Ibid.*, 54.

12   *Ibid.*, 62.

13   *Ibid.*

14   *Ibid.*, 63.

15   *Ibid.*, 64.

16   *Ibid.*, 65.

17   *Ibid.*, xviii.

BIBLIOGRAPHY

Primary Sources

Interviews with disabled persons, representatives of national disabled persons' organisations, rehabilitation professionals and representatives of international non-governmental and UN organisations, 1983–88.

Correspondence with disabled persons, representatives of disabled persons' organisations, representatives of non-governmental and UN organisations, rehabilitation professionals and representatives of uni-disability organisations, 1984–88.

Manuscript collections

Disabled Peoples' International (DPI) Development Office files. DPI, 504–352 Donald Street, Winnipeg, Canada.

Coalition of Provincial Organizations of the Handicapped (COPOH) files. COPOH, 926–294 Portage Avenue, Winnipeg.

Henry Enns, DPI chairperson, files. In possession of Enns.

Society for Manitobans with Disabilities (formerly Society for Crippled Children and Adults of Manitoba), files. SMD, 825 Sherbrook Avenue, Winnipeg.

Periodical and journal articles

Browne, Lois, "Winnipeg congress failed disabled consumers", *Perception* 4 (Sept.-Oct. 1980), 21.

Coalition of Provincial Organizations of the Handicapped (COPOH), "Interview with Georgina Heselton, Saskatchewan Voice of the Handicapped", *Info COPOH* 5 (June 1986), 2.

Combined Disabilities Association, "Eleven Get CDA Loans", *Mainstream: Newsletter of the Combined Disabilities Association, Ltd.* (Sept. 1983), 4.

Cruz, Pedro Roberto, "The General Struggle and the Participation of the Disabled", *Vox Nostra* (Jan. 1988), 9.

Driedger, Diane and April D'Aubin, "Disabled Women: International Profiles", *Caliper* XLI (Mar. 1986), 16–19.

Books

Bowe, F.G., J.E. Jacoby and L.D. Wisemen, *Coalition-Building*, Washington, DC: American Coalition of Citizens with Disabilities (ACCD), 1978.

Chandran-Dudley, Ron (*ed.*), *Disabled Peoples' International Anniversary Journal.*, Singapore: the Author, 1984.

Coalition of Provincial Organizations of the Handicapped (COPOH), *Getting to Know COPOH*. Winnipeg: COPOH, 1985.

Derksen, Jim, *The Disabled Consumer Movement: Policy Implications for Rehabilitation Service Provision*. Winnipeg: COPOH, 1980.

_____(*ed.*), *Report on an Open National Employment Conference*. Winnipeg: COPOH, 1978.

Disabled Peoples' International North America *et al.*, *Trust Betrayed, Hope Denied*. San Francisco: Public Advocates, 1983.

Driedger, Diane (*ed.*), *The Winds of Change: Partners in Development: Proceedings of the Disabled Peoples' International, International Symposium on Development, 1–5 October, 1984, Kingston, Jamaica*. Winnipeg: DPI (Canada), 1985.

Heath, Jeff (*ed.*), *The Adelaide Experience: Report of the First Asia/Pacific Regional Convention of Disabled Peoples' International, Nov., 1984*. Adelaide: DPI (Australia), 1984.

_____(*ed.*), *Developing Leaders: Report of Disabled Peoples' International Leadership Training Course, Adelaide, 1984*. Adelaide: DPI (Australia), 1984.

_____(*ed.*), *'When others Speak for You, You Lose', Proceedings of the First National Assembly of Disabled Peoples' International (Australia), Melbourne, 1983*. Adelaide: South Australian Chapter of DPI, 1983.

International League of Societies for Persons with Mental Handicap, *What is the International League for Persons with Mental Handicap (ILSMH)?* Brussels: ILSMH, 1984.

Miller, Kathleen S., and Linda M. Chadderdon (*eds*), *A Voice of Our Own, Proceedings of the First World Congress of Disabled Peoples' International, Nov. 30–Dec. 4, 1981, Singapore*. East Lansing, Michigan: University Center for International Rehabilitation, Michigan State University, 1982.

_____, Linda M. Chadderdon and Barbara Duncan (*eds*), *Participation of People with Disabilities: International Perspectives*. East Lansing, Michigan: University Center for International Rehabilitation, Michigan State University, 1981.

Oka, Yukiko (*ed.*), *The Engines Are Ready, Let's Go! Report of DPI Asia/Pacific Leadership Training Seminar, April 20–24, 1983*. Tokyo: DPI Asia/Pacific Regional Council, 1983.

Simpson, Allan J., *Consumer Groups: Their Organization and Function*. Winnipeg: COPOH, 1980.

Secondary Sources

Periodical and journal articles

Adams, Alvin, "The Little People — A Tiny Minority with Big Problems", *Ebony* 20 (Oct. 1965), 104–13.

Association des Paralysés de France, *Faire Face* (Aug. 1983).

Bernstein, Norman R., "Chronic Illness and Impairment", *Psychiatric Clinics of North America* 2 (Aug. 1971), 331–46.

Bundesverband für spastisch, gelähmte und andere Körperbehinderte e.V., *Das Band* (May 1979).

Collingan, John, "WCWB", *The New Beacon* (March 1985), 83.

DeJong, Gerben, "Independent Living: From Social Movement to Analytic Paradigm", *Archives of Physical Medicine and Rehabilitation* 60 (Oct. 1979), 435–46.

"Disabled in the USSR — 'A Miserable Existence' ", *Handicaps Monthly* 136 (Feb. 1982), 35–47.

Dlin, Barney M., Abraham Perlman and Evelyn Ringold, "Psychosexual Response to Ileostomy and Colostomy", *American Journal of Psychiatry* 126 (Sept. 1969), 374–81.

Driedger, Diane, and April D'Aubin, "So You Want to Start an Independent Living Center? A Winnipeg Case Study", *Caliper* XL (Dec. 1985), 14–16.

Finkelstein, Vic, "World Health Organization Meeting, 24–28 June 1985, Netherlands", *British Council of Organizations of Disabled People Newsletter* 3 (Jan. 1986), 4–10.

Eidhammer, A., "Disabled People Must Organize!" *The African Rehabilitation Journal* 2 (July 1985), 2–3.

Enns, Henry, "Canadian Society and Disabled People: Issues for Discussion," *Canada's Mental Health* 40 (Dec. 1981), 14–17, 40.

Fine, Michelle and Adrienne Asch, "Disabled Women: Sexism Without the Pedestal", *Journal of Sociology and Social Welfare* VIII (July 1981), 233–48.

Gardeström, Linnéa, "The Swedish Handicap Movement", *Current Sweden* 7 (Nov. 1978), 1–12.

Husveg, Arne, "World Blind Union Founded — A Victory for Solidarity and Good Sense", *Vox Nostra* 2 (Feb. 1984), 18.

Lenihan, John, "Disabled Americans: A History", *Performance* XXVII (Nov.-Dec. 1976 – Jan. 1977).

McLean, D. John, "Henry Enns Doing His Bit", *Caliper* XXXVIII (Sept. 1983), 14–18.

Miles, Mike, "Why Asia Rejects Western Disability Advice", *Quad Wrangle* (Dec. 1983), 27–9.

Parkes, C. Murray and M.N. Napier, "Psychiatric sequelae for amputation", *British Journal of Hospital Medicine* (Nov. 1970), 610–14.

Ross, Val, "Demanding Access for All", *Maclean's*, April 20, 1981.

Rehabilitation International, "Rehabilitation International: 60 Years as a World Organization", *International Rehabilitation Review* (First Quarter, 1982), 1.

Turner, Ralph H., "The theme of contemporary social movements", *British Journal of Sociology* 20 (Dec., 1969), 390–405.

Ward, Edwin J., "A Message from Edwin J. Ward: The International Ostomy History", *International Ostomy Association Bulletin* (Spring 1980).

"We have just begun", *Handicaps Monthly* (Jan. 1982), 7–25.

Weinburg, Martin S., "The Problems of Midgets and Dwarfs and Organizational Remedies: A Study of the Little People of America", *Journal of Health and Social Behavior* 9 (Mar. 1968), 65–71.

Westfall, Wayne, "Jamaica — And Its Disabled", *CUSO Forum* 2 (Nov. 1984), 4–5.

Zola, Irving Kenneth, "Helping One Another: A Speculative History of the Self-Help Movement", *Archives of Physical and Medical Rehabilitation* 60 (Oct. 1979), 452–6.

Unpublished papers

Andersson, Yerker, "Organizations of the Deaf in Developing Countries and Their Relationship to the World Federation of the Deaf", Plenary Lecture at the X World Congress of the World Federation of the Deaf, Helsinki, July 27, 1987.

Baldwin, John F., "The Emancipation of the Undesirable — The Challenged," Australia, *ca.* 1981.*

Ens, Ted, "From Rehabilitation to Self-Determination: A Redefinition of the Assessment Process of Disabled Persons' Situations and Implications for Intervention", Winnipeg, Canada, 1985.*

Shah, Dr Fatima, "Blind Women in the Region (Asia) — Their Status and Role in Society as well as in the Family", paper presented at Training Seminar for Blind Women, Kuala Lumpur, Malaysia, March 23-April 10, 1981.*

Totsuka, Etsuro, Kantoro Nagano and Junri Ozaki, "Patient's Rights and Consumer Movement", paper presented at 11th IOCU World Congress, Bangkok, Thailand, Dec. 9–14, 1984.*

Zukas, Hale, "CIL History", Berkeley, Calif., 1976.*

Chapters

Driedger, Diane, "Disabled Peoples' International (DPI): An International Self-Help Organization" in Transport Canada (*ed.*), *Mobility in the Global Village: A State-of-the-Art Review of Access to Transportation for Elderly and Disabled Persons.* Ottawa: Minister of Supply and Services Canada, 1986.

————, "Speaking for Ourselves: A History of COPOH on its 10th

Anniversary'' in *Coalition of Provincial Organizations of the Handicapped, 1985-86 Annual Report*, Winnipeg: COPOH, 1986, 17–23.

_____, ''The Struggle for Legitimacy: A History of the Coalition of Provincial Organizations of the Handicapped'' in Aileen Wight-Felske (*ed.*), *Dialogue on Disability*, vol. II, Calgary: University of Calgary Press, forthcoming.

Enns, Henry, ''The Historical Development of Attitudes toward the Handicapped: A Framework for Change'' in David S. Freeman and Barry Trute (*eds*), *Treating Families With Special Needs*, Ottawa: Canadian Association of Social Workers, 1981, 175–85.

Morgan, Robin, and Gloria Steinem, ''The International Crime of Genital Mutilation'' in Gloria Steinem, *Outrageous Acts and Everyday Rebellions*, New York: Holt, Rinehart, Winston, 1983, 292–300.

Zucher, Louis A., and Snow, David A., ''Collective Behavior: Social Movements'' in Morris Rosenburg and Ralph H. Turner (*eds*), *Social Psychology: Sociological Perspectives*, New York: Basic Books, 1981, 447–82.

Books

Benderley, Bergl Lieff, *Dancing Without Music: Deafness in America*. New York: Anchor Press/Doubleday, 1980.

Bowe, Frank, *Handicapping America: Barriers to Disabled People*. New York: Harper and Row, 1978.

Browne, Susan E., Debra Connors and Nanci Stern (*eds*), *With the Power of Each Breath: A Disabled Women's Anthology*. Pittsburgh: Cleis Press, 1986.

Campling, Jo, *Images of Ourselves: Women with Disabilities Talking*. London: Routledge and Kegan Paul, 1981.

Campbell, Majorie Wilkins, *No Compromise: The Story of Colonel Baker and the CNIB*. Toronto: McClelland and Stewart, 1965.

Carlsson, Barbro and Folke, *Social Welfare and Handicap Policy in Sweden*. Stockholm: Swedish Institute, *ca.* 1981.

Carnes, G.D., *Social Justice Through Handicapped Power: Perspectives from England and Sweden*. East Lansing, Michigan: University Center for International Rehabilitation, Michigan State University, 1982.

Chigier, E. (*ed.*), *New Dimensions in Rehabilitation, Based on the XIII Congress of Rehabilitation International, Tel Aviv, June 13–18, 1976*. Tel Aviv: Tcherikover, 1978.

Cleland, Max, *Strong at the Broken Places*. Lincoln, Virginia: Chosen Books, 1980.

Council of World Organizations Interested in the Handicapped, *CWOIH Compendium, 1981*. New York: Rehabilitation International, 1981.

Courbeyre, Jean, *1933-1983, Le parcours de l'Association des Paralysés de France: Cinquante ans de créations au service des personnes handicapées*. Paris: Association des Paralysés de France, 1983.

Crewe, Nancy M., and Irving Kenneth Zola, *Independent Living for Physically Disabled People*. San Francisco: Jossey-Bass, 1983.

D'Aubin, April (*ed.*), *Defining the Parameters of Independent Living*. Winnipeg: COPOH, 1986.

De Blindas Förening, *De Blindas Förening 75 år*. Stockholm: De Blindas Förening, 1964.

Disability Resources Centre (*ed.*), *Into the Streets: A Book by and for Disabled People*. Collingwood, Australia: Disability Resources Centre, 1981.

Edwards, Jean Parker, *We Are People First: Our Handicaps are Secondary*. Portland, Oregon: EDNICK, 1982.

Finkelstein, Vic, *Attitudes and Disabled People: Issues for Discussion*. New York: World Rehabilitation Fund, 1980.

Freire, Paulo, *Pedagogy of the Oppressed* (transl. Myra Bergman Ramos). New York: Seabury Press, 1970.

————, *The Politics of Education: Culture, Power and Liberation* (transl. by Donaldo Macedo). Mass.: Bergin and Garvey, 1985.

Fudge, Derek, and Holmes, Patty, *Together for Social Change: Employing Disabled Canadians*. Ottawa: National Union of Public and Government Employees and COPOH, 1983.

Glick, Ferne Pellman, *Breaking Silence: A Family Grows with Deafness*. Scottdale, Penn.: Herald Press, 1982.

Goffman, Erving, *Stigma: Notes on the Management of Spoiled Identity*. Englewood Cliffs, NJ: Prentice-Hall, 1963.

Habeck, Rochelle V. *et al.* (*eds*), *Economics and Equity in Employment of People with Disabilities: International Policies and Practices*. East Lansing, Michigan: University Center for International Rehabilitation, Michigan State University, 1985.

Hammerman, Susan, and Stephen Maikowski (*eds*), *The Economics of Disability: International Perspectives*. New York: Rehabilitation International, 1981.

Harry, Gerard, *Man's Miracle: The Story of Helen Keller and her European Sisters*. New York: Doubleday, Page, 1913.

Health and Welfare Canada, *Disabled Persons in Canada*. Ottawa: Minister of Supply and Services Canada, 1980.

Helander, E., P. Mendis and G. Nelson, *Training the Disabled in the Community: An Experimental Manual on Rehabilitation and Disability Prevention for Developing Countries*. Geneva: World Health Organization, 1980.

Hummel, Barbara, and Gilpatrick, Anthonette, *Peer Support Training Manual*. Wisconsin: Access to Independence, 1984.

Independent Living Resource Center, *Independent Living for Persons with Disabilities in Canada*. Winnipeg: Independent Living Resource Center, 1985.

Killilea, Marie, *Karen*. Englewood Cliffs, NJ: Prentice-Hall, 1952.

King, Mike, *The Mike King Story*. Intercourse, Penn.: Good Books, 1985.

Kleinfeld, Sonny, *The Hidden Minority: A Profile of Handicapped Americans*. Boston: Little, Brown, 1979.

Linedecker, Clifford, with Michael and Maureen Ryan, *Kerry: Agent Orange and an American Family*. New York: St Martin's Press, 1982.

Marlett, Nancy J., Robert S. Gall and Aileen Wight-Felske (*eds*), *Dialogue on Disability: A Canadian Perspective*, vol. I: *The Service System*. Calgary: University of Calgary Press, 1984.

Matthews, Gwyneth Ferguson, *Voices from the Shadows: Women with Disabilities Speak Out*. Toronto: Women's Educational Press, 1983.

Mauss, Armand L, *Social Problems as Social Movements*. Philadelphia: J.B. Lippincott, 1975.

National Council for the Disabled, *Associations and Societies of the Disabled in Sweden Directory*. Stockholm: National Council for the Disabled, 1984.

Neufeldt, Aldred H. (*ed.*), *Celebrating Differences*. Newton, Kansas: Faith and Life Press,1984.

Ohsberg, H. Oliver, *The Church and Persons with Handicaps*. Scottdale, Penn.: Herald Press, 1982.

Richert, Val Regehr, *Moving In . . . A Housing Manual*. Winnipeg: Independent Living Resource Center, 1985.

Schaefer, Nicola, *Does She Know She's There?* Toronto: Fitzhenry and Whiteside, 1978.

Special Parliamentary Committee on the Handicapped and Disabled. *Obstacles: The Third Report*. Ottawa: Minister of Supply and Services Canada, 1981.

Swedish Institute, *Support for the Disabled in Sweden*. Stockholm: Swedish Institute, 1981.

Swedish International Development Authority, *The Women's Dimension in Development Assistance: SIDA's Plan of Action*. Stockholm: SIDA Office of Women in Development, 1985.

Turner, Ralph H., and Louis M. Killian, *Collective Behavior*, 2nd edn, Englewood Cliffs, NJ: Prentice-Hall, 1972.

United Nations, *World Program of Action Concerning Disabled Persons*. New York: United Nations, 1983.

Valens, Evans G., *A Long Way Up: The Story of Jill Kinmont*. New York: Harper and Row, 1966.

Wolfensberger, Wolf, *Normalization: The Principle of Normalization in Human Services*. Toronto: National Institute on Mental Retardation, 1972.

---

*The author's possession.

INDEX